CHEESE SWEETS AND SAVORIES

Pies,
Cheesecakes,
Quiches,
Appetizers

CHEESE SWEETS AND SAVORIES

Pies, Cheesecakes, Quiches, Appetizers

By Steve Sherman

The Stephen Greene Press
Brattleboro, Vermont
Lexington, Massachusetts

FIRST EDITION

Copyright © 1982 by Steve Sherman

This book was manufactured in the United States of America. It is designed by Irving Perkins Associates and published by The Stephen Greene Press, Fessenden Road, Brattleboro, Vermont 05301.

Library of Congress Cataloging in Publication Data

Sherman, Steve, 1938–
  Cheese sweets and savories.

  Includes index.
  1. Cheesecake (Cookery)   2. Quiches (Cookery)
3. Cookery (Cheese)   I. Title.
TX773.S428   641.8′653   81-23778
ISBN 0-8289-0464-2   AACR2

CONTENTS

Introduction 1

The Sweets

The Savories

INTRODUCTION

Without doubt, cheesecakes come with a distinctive tone that other desserts plainly lack. At times the tone is vogueish and faddy, at other times great and grand; and if a classic recipe is brilliantly executed and magnificently presented, well, it's glory.

What gives cheesecakes such a sweeping reputation? It can only be their sumptuous appeal and charismatic taste, their sturdy presence, their uninhibited festivity, their princely obviousness, their democratic diversity. The variety of reasons supports the variety of recipes. Whatever the cause, the bottom line is this: Cheesecakes command attention.

CHEESE SWEETS

YEARS AGO at a special occasion I gravitated to two perfect toast-colored New York–style cheesecakes propped center stage on a buffet table. I devoured more than was inconspicuous, and asked from what bakery these delicious cakes were bought. "We made them ourselves," came the answer. Blazing insight. Such creations could be prepared in home kitchens and didn't need the *toque blanche* of the professional chef at all.

So began fifteen years of baking cheesecakes—not every day, but frequently enough to assure me that I could never be bored with them. The range of recipes in this book shows at a glance the endless variety of cheesecake. No longer should cheesecake be equated only with the familiar New York style or the quick sour cream-topped cheese pie, both delectable, to be sure, but not the end of the line. Variations on the theme of cheese are virtually unlimited—from the purity of coeur à la crème to the chocolate almond rum cheesecake, from whipped cream to yogurt recipes. They take the form of pyramid molds, as in the paskha; the shape of cheese rounds, as in Lindy's; the slant-edge of pies, as in the fruit and low-fat renditions; the upright crusts of tarts. Their methods of creation vary from cooked to uncooked, blender to hand-mixed, single to triple layers. Their tastes spin out into unleashed imagination—spicy, spirit-tasting, nutty, creamy, sweet, tangy. They come from Russia, Mexico, Greece, Italy, France, Finland, Israel, Hungary, Germany.

In short, cheesecakes line up in a spectrum of cooking techniques and tastes. With all their variety, too, the added appeal is that cheesecakes may be the most classicly simple and yet the most alluring dessert of them all.

SINCE THE GREEKS

THE ANCIENT Greeks had a variety of cheesecakes, which they prized so much that they served them as wedding cakes. At Argos the custom was for the bride to bring roasted cheesecakes covered with honey for the wedding guests. Plato mentions cheesecakes, the island of Samos was noted for cheesecakes, Aristophanes heralded them.

In his work *De Agricultura,* Cato the Elder (died 149 B.C.) gives us this Roman recipe for sweet-wine cheesecake: "Moisten 1 peck of wheat flour with must. Add aniseed, cumin, 2 lb. of fat, 1 lb. of cheese, and some grated bark of a laurel twig. Shape and place each cake on a bay-leaf; then bake."

As Barbara Flower and Elisabeth Rosenbaum tell us in their translation of his cookbook, Marcus Gavius Apicius in the first century A.D. went a step further. He took Cato's cheesecakes and steeped them in milk, heated them up slightly in an oven, poured honey over them, sprinkled them with pepper, and served them.

Athenaeus, a Greek writer who lived in Rome toward the end of the second century A.D., wrote a masterwork of fifteen volumes titled *Deipnosophistai* ("Sophists at Dinner"; or, if you prefer, "Connoisseurs in Dining," "Banquet of the Learned"). In it he gives us this recipe for cheesecake: "Take some cheese and pound it, put in a brazen sieve and strain it, then add honey and flour made from spring wheat, and heat the whole together into one mass." It's worth a try for antiquity's sake.

Apicius was the one who left us with what is considered the earliest extant cookbook, called *De Re Coquinaria* ("Of Culinary Matters"). He was such a devotee of good food that not only did a fine table mean to him the good life, it meant life itself. When the money he spent on his extravagant meals dwindled toward an intolerable future, Apicius poisoned himself. Such consuming devotion to high living, and the means to indulge it, fulfill our image of the Roman delight of the senses. Part of this delight was cheese, which was plentiful throughout the empire and in many forms, including soft thin cheese with which to make many dishes. One inherited Roman recipe was named *Tyropatinam* ("a dish with cheese"). It called for cooking milk, eggs, honey, and pepper, and was in reality a custard.

The Harleian manuscripts in the British Museum mention a medieval cheesecake made with brie, six egg yolks, saffron, and spices—a rich, honored concoction of an ill-reputed age. The Middle Ages were a time of surprisingly inviting dishes, although quality control in medieval years fell short of the feeblest recognition.

In 1390 the French *darioll* was mentioned in *The Forme of Cury,* a book of the cooks of England's Richard II. (*Cury* was the Old English word for cooking.) The little cheesecakes were spelled *daryols* in the book. The original recipe went as follows: "Take creme of cowe mylke, (or) almands. Do thereto ayren (eggs), with sugar, safron, and salt. Medle it ifere (mix it together). Do it in a coffyn of two ynche depe; bake it wel, and serve it forth." The tiny pleasing cheese tarts became known as Richmond Maids of Honor. They were prepared by Queen Elizabeth's maids of honor at her Richmond palace. Evidently, as early as Chaucer's time *daryol* was a word meaning "maid of honor." The dariole also appeared in 1653 in LaVarenne's *Le Pastissier François,* and in 1739 in Menon's *Nouveau Traite de la Cuisine.*

Cheesecakes continued to be baked and enjoyed through the centuries until they reached America, where they found a most loyal and receptive palate. Americans eat more cheesecake than any other peoples. Perhaps it is because of our abundance of dairy products; or maybe it comes from the widespread use of simple custards made on the frontiers that led to more involved cheesecakes. The most likely reason is that Americans recognize the rich simplicity of a cake that may be so widely adapted and modified.

CHEESE SAVORIES

ANOTHER POPULAR dish is a cheese pie served as an appetizer or entrée. Not only are these cheesy custard tarts tasty, but somehow they're entertaining as well. Their presentation may be formal or casual, their ingredients rich or light, their style exotic or familiar. They are, in short, supremely versatile and always welcome.

Originally, the quiches of Lorraine, France, are said not to have contained cheese at all but merely eggs, bacon, cream, and seasonings. With the addition of cheese and onions or scallions, the concept opened the imagination to myriad possibilities and broadened the meaning of the word *quiche* itself.

Today, quiches include an appetizing array of cheeses and vegetables. Each one displays its own complementary seasonings for the highlighted ingredients. In the second part of this book you'll find old favorite combinations blended into cheese mixtures and crusts—bacon and tomato, ham and leek, black bean and rice. You'll also find an irresistible creamy spinach quiche, a hearty chick pea and lentil quiche, an easy-eating eggplant and tomato quiche.

Besides the quiches and cheese pies (what is the difference but élan?), cheese-based recipes without a crust share the pages. These include the classic Swiss fondue, the French gougère, the Mexican tamale pie, the Italian gnocchi verde, and other dishes that use cheese with either a gypsy flair or a ballerina's grace.

CHEESE

THE AUTHENTIC origin of cheese is linked to the legend of the Arab who carried milk in a goat's stomach on his camel trip across the hot desert. Churning in the heat, and being subject to rennet in the stomach lining, the milk curdled by separating the whey from the curd. The result: cheese.

This in its most fundamental form is the process of cheese-making today. Milk (just about any kind, from cow to yak) is heated, curdled, washed, dried, pressed, and aged. What kind of milk is used, how long it is cooked, at what temperature, what bacteria dominate in the milk, how long the cheese is aged, under what conditions and at what temperature, how much salt is added, whether coloring or seasonings are added, and many other factors, all determine the type of cheese produced. Whatever the end product, cheese is a milk curd, derives its name from the Latin *caseus,* and has the phosphoprotein casein as its base. The muscle-building casein in milk and cheese cannot be found elsewhere.

In the world of cheesecake, cheese refers mostly to cream cheese. Cheddar, cottage cheese, ricotta, and the Swiss-type cheeses are used frequently in quiches. Many cheeses may be made at home, including some used for cheesecakes, although most likely you'll purchase them at the market. However, for purity and freshness, making your own cheesecake cheeses is worth at least one easy attempt (which may convince you to make them more often). Ricotta is a whey-extracted cheese, the making of which is based on the premise that nothing should be wasted. An overwhelming and impractical amount of whey is needed to make enough authentic ricotta at home for a small-sized cheesecake. Better to buy the ricotta produced by large dairy producers, which by and large use whole milk. Best of all is to buy the delicate, dry, whey-based ricotta found at some Italian markets.

Cottage cheese, on the other hand, is extremely simple to make at home. It is made from skim milk or instant nonfat dehydrated milk. The following recipe makes a convenient one pound. If you need more, simply double it.

COTTAGE CHEESE

½ gallon skim milk
⅓ C buttermilk
⅛ rennet tablet
¼ C water
 salt and cream to taste

1. Mix skim milk and buttermilk in an enamel or stainless steel container. Dissolve rennet in water and add to milk. Heat to lukewarm, remove from burner, and let it set in a warm place for 10–12 hours or until it curdles into a smooth custardy texture. (You can make cottage cheese in 1 hour by using ½ rennet tablet for the above ingredients, but watch carefully not to curdle the milk too hard before proceeding to the second step.)

2. With a long sharp knife cut the cheese in a crisscross pattern into small cubes about a half inch or smaller.
3. Heat the curds very slowly. Never let them boil or come close to boiling. It takes 30 minutes or longer to turn the curds into firmer familiar-looking granules. Test these by running cold water over some curds and taste (they'll be properly acid-tasting).
4. When the cheese reaches a preferred texture, drain the whey from the curds through a cheesecloth-lined colander or sieve. Rinse the curds thoroughly under lukewarm water and then cold water.
5. Place curds in bowl and salt to taste. Add cream to taste. Chill.

Making cream cheese is simpler. These recipes make about half a pound.

CREAM CHEESE I

2 C heavy cream
2 T buttermilk
   salt to taste

1. Add buttermilk to cream. Heat to lukewarm.
2. Place in cloth bag to drain over a plate, or place in a covered enamel or glass bowl to set. This takes 24 hours or more.
3. Remove cheese from bag, or skim cheese from bowl.
4. Place in bowl and salt to taste, if you wish. Place in covered bowl and chill.

CREAM CHEESE II

½ C heavy cream
2 C whole milk
1 C yogurt
   salt to taste

1. Blend cream, milk, and yogurt.
2. Bring slowly to lukewarm temperature and let stand uncovered in warm place for 10–12 hours or until thickened.
3. Line a colander or sieve with double-layered cheesecloth and place the cheese in it to drain.
4. Tie the cheesecloth around cheese and suspend it so that the cheese may drain slowly.
5. When the cheese is set, remove from cheesecloth and chill.

Cream cheese made at home is very soft at room temperature and normally cannot be formed into a solid brick shape. To do this, commercial makers add vegetable gum.

Cream cheese makes a delicious crust, but it is extremely rich.

CREAM CHEESE CRUST

½ C sweet butter
3 oz. cream cheese, softened
1 C unbleached all-purpose flour
⅛ t salt

1. Cream butter and cheese.
2. Mix flour and salt. Gradually blend into cheese mixture. Cover and chill for 3–4 hours.
3. Quickly roll out ⅛-inch thick on floured board. Place in 9-inch pie plate. Pierce with fork.
4. Bake at 450 degrees F. for 7–9 minutes or until lightly toasted. Makes 1 crust.

INGREDIENTS AND EQUIPMENT

GOOD CHEESE is the first step in producing good cheesecakes. Just as the freshest minds produce the most enjoyable conversations or works of art, so do the freshest ingredients produce the best cheesecakes. Freshly grated orange zest, freshly grated nutmeg, unadulterated milk, fresh eggs, fresh flour, fresh seasonings all help the reach for perfection.

Also, try to work with cheese at room temperature. This leads to increased lightness of texture and makes a noticeable difference. Eggs at room temperature also produce better results. (*Tip:* A hurried way to get packaged cream cheese and eggs to room temperature is to immerse them in warm water.)

In general, certain crusts should be prepared by cutting sweet butter, shortening, or lard into the crumbs or flour with two knives. Try to avoid mashing the butter and flour with your fingers or a wire pastry cutter. These latter two methods tend to compress the dough into heavy solids, and end up producing a tougher crust. If you take the extra couple of minutes with the knives, plus lightly rolling the dough and lightly placing it into the pan or plate, your crusts bake lighter.

Cheesecakes, pies, quiches, and appetizers are best baked in springform pans, tart or flan pans, and pie plates. A springform pan has a side rim that pressure-snaps closed, sealing the rim to the removable bottom. A cake in a springform may be placed on a platter, and then the rim unsnapped and removed without transferring the cake from the baking pan bottom. If you bake a crustless cake, it's wise to place the springform pan on a large baking sheet to avoid any chance of having the unset filling seep through and drip onto the oven bottom.

Tart and flan pans are interchangeable; a separate bottom rests inside the pan rim. A standard way to remove a cake from a tart pan is to place the pan over a glass. Then by gently lowering the rim, you leave the bottom baking sheet resting on the glass, which supports the cake so that it may be transferred to a serving platter. Beyond springform and tart pans, the cheesecake-maker needs no special equipment other than what a conventionally-equipped kitchen would have already.

USING THIS BOOK

IN THE first half of the book, all the sweets—cakes and pies—are alphabetically arranged by distinctive ingredient or by common name. The index cross-references them. In the second half, the savories—the quiches and other cheese-based dishes—are arranged likewise. All entries are presented in as clear a format as possible, and all suggest the freshest ingredients available.

Above all, take to heart that these recipes are guidelines, not regulations. Add, subtract, and invent when the maverick urge bubbles forth. Cooking requires much science to get food to the table, but cooking sparks to life through art. Pay attention to the rules of science when you bake a few of these dishes, but by all means let the suggestions here be springboards for your own personal touches, whims, and flourishes. Cooking may be scientific, but the art is the fun.

THE SWEETS

**Cheesecakes,
Cheese Pies
and
Cheese Tarts**

Almond Cheesecake

CRUST:

1½ C chocolate wafer crumbs
1   C blanched almonds, lightly
    toasted and ground
6   T sweet butter, melted, and
    butter for pan

CAKE:

1½ lbs. cream cheese, softened
1   C sugar
4   large eggs
⅓   C heavy cream
¼   C almond-flavored liqueur
1   t vanilla extract

TOPPING:

2   C sour cream
1   T sugar
1   t vanilla extract
    slivered almonds, blanched
        and toasted

1. For crust, combine crumbs, almonds, and butter. Press mixture onto the bottom and side of a buttered 9-inch springform pan.
2. For cake, cream together cheese and sugar.
3. Beat in eggs one at a time.
4. Add cream, liqueur, and vanilla, and beat until light.
5. Pour batter into crust. Bake at 350 degrees F. for 30 minutes or until center is set.
6. Remove the cake from the oven and let it stand for 5 minutes.
7. For topping, combine sour cream, sugar, and vanilla. Spread mixture evenly on the cake. Return cake to oven for 5–7 minutes or until topping is set.
8. Cool cake on a wire rack. Then chill it.
9. Place the cake on a platter and remove the pan rim. Sprinkle toasted blanched slivered almonds decoratively over the top. Serves 10–12.

Dark chocolate wafer crusts always make a startling contrast with a white sour cream top—a visual extra, along with the irresistible taste. Almond tastes are in all three parts of this striking cake, which is good for a semi-formal dinner party. Almonds have long been a symbol of faithfulness and generosity, two attributes that match classic cheesecake recipes.

Almond Cheese Pie

CRUST:

1½ C unbleached all-purpose
    flour
½ t salt
½ C sweet butter
2–3 T cream sherry

FILLING:

1 C dry ricotta
8 oz. cream cheese, softened
¼ lb. toasted blanched
    almonds, finely chopped
2 large eggs
⅔ C sugar
1 t vanilla extract

1. For crust, mix flour and salt. Cut in butter. Stir in sherry (and cold water if needed) one T at a time until dough forms a ball. Roll out and line a 9-inch pie plate. Cut remaining dough into strips ½-inch wide for lattice topping.
2. For filling, blend ricotta with cream cheese.
3. Combine cheeses with almonds.
4. Beat eggs with sugar until frothy. Stir in vanilla. Add to cheeses and blend well.
5. Pour into crust. Place lattice strips over top.
6. Bake at 350 degrees F. for 45 minutes, or until center is set and lattice is lightly toasted. Cool. Sprinkle with confectioners' sugar before serving. Serves 6.

Place the lattice strips very gently over the pie so that it doesn't absorb them or allow them to sink too much into the filling. The ricotta makes this a light-tasting version.

Almond Peach Cheesecake

FILLING:
1 lb. can of peaches, drained
1 T sugar
2 t cornstarch dissolved in 1 T water (optional)

CAKE:
½ C blanched ground almonds
¼ lb. sweet butter
½ C plus 2 T sugar
1 lb. cream cheese, softened
¼ C unbleached all-purpose flour
4 eggs, separated
⅓ C all-purpose cream, lightly whipped
¼ t almond extract

TOPPING:
2 T light brown sugar
1 t ground coriander
¼ C blanched ground almonds

1. For filling, purée peaches in blender. Pour into saucepan, add sugar, and cook until thickened. Stir in cornstarch mixture, if needed to thicken. Cool and set aside.
2. For cake, blanch ¾ C almonds (boil them a minute, drain, remove skins). Dry and grind in blender or food processor. Set aside.
3. Cream butter and sugar.
4. Add cream cheese and flour to butter mixture and blend.
5. Stir in egg yolks one at a time.
6. Add cream and extract.
7. Beat egg whites until stiff but not dry. Fold in half of whites at a time.
8. Fold in ½ C almonds.
9. In 8-inch springform pan spread less than half of batter on bottom. Then carefully spread on peach purée. Spread rest of batter carefully over filling.
10. Mix all topping ingredients and sprinkle on top.
11. Bake at 325 degrees F. for 60–70 minutes or until center is set. Turn off heat and keep cake in oven for another hour. Cool before removing pan rim. Serves 8.

The unexpected taste of the hidden peach filling makes a delicious surprise. Yet neither the peach nor almond tastes unbalance the overall harmony of these two complementary flavors. This is a rich cake, but beating the egg whites produces a lighter, easily devourable texture. The center may sink when cooling, but not too much if you cook the cake long enough to compensate for the moisture of the purée.

Apple Cheddar Pie

CRUST:
1⅓ C unbleached all-purpose
    flour
1   t salt
½   C sweet butter
4   T cold milk

FILLING:
6   large cooking apples,
    peeled, cored, sliced
1¼ C sugar, divided
2   T lemon juice
1   t vanilla extract
½   t cinnamon
2   C shredded Cheddar cheese
2–3 T confectioners' sugar

1. For crust, combine flour and salt. Cut in butter. Stir in milk one T at a time until dough forms a ball. Chill.

2. For filling, combine apple slices, ½ C sugar, lemon juice, and vanilla. Let set for 10–15 minutes. Then drain apples.

3. Butter an 8-inch cast iron skillet. Sprinkle ¾ C sugar on bottom. Arrange apples in overlapping circles. Press apples down.

4. Sprinkle on cinnamon and cheese.

5. Roll dough in a circle of about 9½ inches in diameter. Place over apples. Tuck edges into skillet. Pierce crust with fork.

6. Cook over medium heat on top of stove for 5 minutes.

7. Place skillet on baking sheet and bake at 450 degrees F. for about 30 minutes or until crust is brown.

8. Remove from oven and let rest about 5 minutes. Place large serving platter over tart and quickly turn skillet over. The tart should fall from the skillet, apple-side up. Cool. Decoratively sprinkle on thin layer of confectioners' sugar. Serves 6–8.

This *tarte tatin* marries two traditional go-together foods with a flair—apples and Cheddar cheese. Northern Spy apples are perfect for this. They're tart and meaty and have a hearty apple taste.

Apple Prune Cheese Tart

CRUST:

1	C unbleached all-purpose flour
½	t salt
⅓	C shortening
4	T all-purpose cream

FILLING:

1	C prunes, cooked, pitted
3	T sugar
1¼	C shredded sharp Cheddar cheese
2	large eggs, slightly beaten
½	C all-purpose cream
2	cooking apples, peeled, cored, sliced
2–3	T sweet butter
¼	C sugar
½	t allspice
½	t cinnamon

1. For crust, mix flour and salt. Cut in shortening. Stir in cream one T at a time until dough forms a ball. Chill 10 minutes. Roll out and place in a 9-inch tart pan. Pierce with fork. Bake at 450 degrees F. for 7–9 minutes, or until lightly toasted. Cool.
2. For filling, mash the prune pulp.
3. Stir in the sugar. Spread the prune mixture over the crust.
4. Sprinkle the cheese over the prune mixture.
5. Mix the eggs and cream. Pour over the cheese.
6. Arrange the apple slices decoratively by overlapping them partially in a circle around the edge of the crust and another smaller circle in the center.
7. Dot the apples with butter.
8. Combine the sugar, allspice, and cinnamon. Sprinkle over the top.
9. Bake at 350 degrees F. for 25 minutes or until the top is well-toasted. Serves 6.

The original Cheddar cheese was born in a village of the same name near Bristol, England. Today in this country good Cheddar, such as that from Vermont, ranks with other high quality cheese and shouldn't be taken for granted because of its familiarity. Pairing good Cheddar with good apples, such as Northern Spy or Greenings, and underpinning them with a sweetened prune purée, as here, makes for a good robust wintry taste.

Apple Rum Cheese Pie

CRUST:
- 1 C unbleached all-purpose flour
- ½ t salt
- 2 T sweet butter
- 3 T vegetable shortening
- 3–4 T cold milk

FILLING:
- 3 cooking apples, sliced, mashed (not puréed)
- ⅓ C sugar
- 8 oz. cream cheese, softened
- 2 large eggs
- ½ C light cream
- 3 T dark rum

1. For crust, mix flour and salt. Cut in butter and shortening. Stir in milk one T at a time until dough forms a ball. Chill. Roll out and place in a 9-inch pie plate. Pierce with fork. Bake at 450 degrees F. for 7–9 minutes or until lightly toasted.
2. For filling, spread apples over crust.
3. Cream sugar into cheese.
4. Beat in eggs one at a time.
5. Stir in cream and rum. Pour mixture over apples.
6. Bake at 350 degrees F. for 30 minutes or until center is set. Serves 6.

Rum and apples together have warmed many a cold New England body in winter. The "comfortable waters of Barbados," as rum was called, originally was made from fermented molasses, although many rums today get their darkness from caramel coloring. This dish makes a rich detour from the usual apple pie, and is especially good during the height of the late fall harvest season.

Apricot Almond Cheesecake Julia

MERINGUE:

- 1   C almonds, blanched, toasted, finely ground
- ⅔ C sugar
- 1½ T cornstarch
- 5   large egg whites
     butter and flour for baking pan

FILLING:

- 8   oz. cream cheese, softened
- ⅓ C heavy cream
- 1   C (fully packed) dried apricots, cooked, puréed
- ⅔ C confectioners' sugar
     grated rind of 1 fresh lemon

ICING:

- 1   C confectioners' sugar
- 3   T water
- 1   egg white
- ¼ t fresh cream of tartar
     dash of salt
- ¼ t almond extract

1. For meringue, reserve 2 T ground almonds. To rest add sugar and cornstarch.

2. Beat egg whites until stiff but not dry. Carefully fold almond mixture into whites.

3. Very generously butter two 8-inch cake pans. Coat with flour.

4. Pour half of almond mixture into each pan. Smooth top. Bake meringues at 300 degrees F. for 40 minutes or until they are slightly brown and their sides pull away from pan. Remove from pan and cool.

5. For filling, cut cream cheese into cubes and place in bowl. Add cream and beat until smooth and light.

6. To apricot purée, add confectioners' sugar and lemon rind.

7. Combine cheese and apricot mixtures.

8. To assemble, place one meringue upside down on plate. Spread half of apricot mixture on top. Place second meringue upright on top of mixture. Spread rest of apricot evenly on top only.

9. For icing, boil sugar in water until dissolved. Pouring over blend of egg white, cream of tartar, and salt, beat with electric mixer until firm. Beat in almond extract.

10. Spread icing evenly only around sides of cake, joining edge of top apricot mixture.

11. Sprinkle reserved almond powder over side and top of cake. Chill. Serves 10–12.

A variation of a *dacquoise,* this cake tastes as it looks—simple but elegant. The apricot pastel on top, set against the snow white icing on the sides, suggests a special Sunday brunch or the end to an effervescent summer dinner. Eating a slice of this ambrosia confirms it.

Apricot Cheese Pie

CRUST:

1⅛ C graham cracker crumbs
¾ t allspice
4 T sweet butter, melted

FILLING:

8 oz. cream cheese, softened
1 15-oz. can sweetened
   condensed milk
⅓ C lemon juice
½ t vanilla extract
6–8 canned whole pitted
   apricots, drained and
   halved (reserve syrup)
¼ C sugar
1½ T cornstarch
   dash of salt
½ C apricot syrup
½ C strained orange juice

1. For crust, mix crumbs and allspice. Stir in butter to moisten mixture thoroughly. Press crumbs evenly into 9-inch pie plate. Bake at 450 degrees F. for 4 minutes or until set. Cool.
2. For filling, beat cream cheese until fluffy. Add milk slowly, beating well. Stir in lemon juice and vanilla.
3. Pour into crust and chill for 2–3 hours until set.
4. Carefully place apricot halves decoratively on top of cake.
5. In saucepan mix sugar, cornstarch, and salt. Stir in reserved apricot syrup and orange juice. Mix until well blended. Cook over medium heat, stirring constantly until thick and clear. Cook for additional 2–3 minutes. Cool.
6. Pour cooled glaze over apricots. Chill for 2 hours. Serves 6–8.

Except for the crust, this pie requires no baking or gelatin. The lemon juice and sugared milk react to thicken and set the pie. Instead of placing the apricot halves round side up (sometimes making them look like egg yolks at first glance), arrange them with the round side down. Then set a choice blueberry into each before glazing.

Apricot Prune Cheesecake

CRUST:
- 1 C lemon wafer crumbs
- ¼ C sweet butter, melted

FILLING:
- 2 C medium prunes, cooked, pitted
- 1 C dried apricots, cooked, puréed
- 1 T brown sugar
- 1 C cottage cheese, sieved
- 8 oz. cream cheese, softened
- 3 large eggs
- ½ C evaporated milk
- 1 T lemon juice
- ¾ C sugar
- ⅓ C unbleached all-purpose flour

1. For crust, mix crumbs and butter. Press into bottom and partially up side of an 8-inch springform pan. Chill. Bake at 450 degrees F. for 4 minutes or until set. Cool.

2. For filling, mash prunes and set aside.

3. Mix apricots and brown sugar. Set aside.

4. Combine cottage cheese and cream cheese and beat until soft. Beat in eggs one at a time.

5. Blend in milk, lemon juice, and sugar. Whisk in flour until thoroughly blended.

6. Spread prunes on bottom of crust. Pour in cheese filling. Bake at 325 degrees F. for 40 minutes. Turn off heat and keep oven door closed for 15 minutes more. Remove from oven and cool.

7. Spread apricot purée evenly on top of cake. Cool. Serves 8–10.

This is a moist way of using two dried fruits. It also presents a colorful slice with the dark prunes on the bottom, rich orange-colored apricots on top, and the creamy-white cake in the middle. Serving at room temperature brings out the full fruit flavors.

Apricot Prune Cheese Tart

CRUST:

1   C lemon cookie crumbs
¼   C sweet butter, melted, and butter for pan

FILLING:

1   C dried apricots, rehydrated
1   C dried prunes, rehydrated, pitted
⅓   lb. brie cheese, de-crusted, softened
½   C ricotta
¾   C sugar
2   large eggs, slightly beaten grated rind of 1 lemon
¾   t allspice

1. For crust, stir crumbs and butter together. Chill. Press into 9-inch buttered tart pan. Bake at 450 degrees F. for 4 minutes or until set. Cool.

2. For filling, prepare apricots and prunes. Set aside.

3. With wooden spoon blend brie and ricotta until smooth.

4. Beat in sugar and eggs.

5. Stir in lemon rind and allspice.

6. Pour into crust. Gently place apricots on filling in a circle around the tart edge. Place prunes in a circle inside the apricots. Repeat circles until filling is covered.

7. Bake at 350 degrees F. for 25 minutes or until center of cheese mixture is set. Serves 6.

A gentle way to rehydrate the dried apricots and prunes is to place them in separate bowls well covered with water overnight. This avoids the chance of overcooking or bruising them if you boil the fruit to rehydrate. Served with sweetened whipped cream dusted with coriander, this makes a colorful dish with a big rainbow of tastes.

Banana Cheese Pie

CRUST:
1   C graham cracker crumbs
    (reserve 1 T)
¼   C sweet butter, melted

FILLING:
1   T unflavored gelatin
½   C water
2   large eggs, separated
½   C sugar
8   oz. cream cheese, softened
1   T lemon juice
    dash of salt
1   C sour cream
3   ripe bananas, sliced (reserve
    a few slices)

1. For crust, mix crumbs and butter together. Press onto bottom and side of 9-inch pie plate. Bake at 450 degrees F. for 4 minutes or until set. Cool.

2. For filling, briefly soak gelatin in ¼ C water.

3. Meanwhile, combine egg yolks with sugar and ¼ C water and cook in double boiler until thickened, stirring constantly. Remove from heat and mix in gelatin.

4. In separate bowl, beat cheese until light and fluffy.

5. Add the gelatin mixture, lemon juice, and salt. Beat well. Fold in the sour cream.

6. Beat the egg whites until stiff and fold into the cheese mixture. Refrigerate for 20–30 minutes until partially set, stirring regularly.

7. To assemble, begin and end with cheese mixture. Alternate layers of cheese with sliced bananas. Place reserved slices decoratively on center top. Sprinkle reserved crumbs around inside rim of pie. Chill 2–3 hours. Serves 6.

Most of the time it's a good idea to garnish the top of a pie or cake with one of the main ingredients inside, as is done with this pie. This prepares the taste buds and keeps the integrity of both the cook and eater intact. You might dip the garnish banana slices in lemon juice first for added zest and to help prevent them from darkening. This pie proves that easy-to-prepare can go along with good-to-eat.

Beer and Cheddar Cheesecake

CRUST:

1½   C graham cracker crumbs
¼   C sweet butter, melted, and
        butter for pan

FILLING:

2   lb. cream cheese, softened
1¼   C sugar
4   large eggs
1   t lemon juice
½   C beer
1⅓   C shredded Cheddar cheese
½   C heavy cream, slightly
      whipped

1. For crust, combine crumbs with butter. Press on bottom and side of buttered 8-inch springform pan.
2. For filling, beat cream cheese until soft. Beat in sugar.
3. Add eggs one at a time, beating very well.
4. Add lemon juice, beer, and cheese. Mix thoroughly.
5. Fold in cream.
6. Pour the mixture into the crust. Bake at 300 degrees F. for 1½–2 hours or until center is set (cake will color golden).
7. Turn off heat and allow cake to remain in oven with the door slightly open to let the heat out gradually. Remove from oven and cool in kitchen. Chill before serving. Serves 12.

The unlikely ingredient of beer in a cheesecake may at first sound unappetizing, but the cake will surprise you with its delicious cheesy, slightly tangy taste. This version calls for a generous supply of beer. The neighborly Cheddar taste balances the beer perfectly. Slow cooking keeps this a moderately light-textured cake. Slices may be served at room temperature, but chilling it first brings out the beer flavor, which is the entire point.

Blackberry Jam Cheese Pie

CRUST:
1 C unbleached all-purpose
    flour
½ t salt
2 T sweet butter
3 T vegetable shortening
3–4 T cold milk

FILLING:
    blackberry jam
1 lb. ricotta
2 egg yolks
½ C sugar
1 t vanilla extract
¼ C sweet butter, melted
½ C black currants

TOPPING:
2 egg whites
¼ C sugar
2 egg yolks
3 T unbleached all-purpose
    flour
    confectioners' sugar

1. For crust, mix flour and salt. Cut in butter and shortening. Stir in milk one T at a time to form dough into ball. Roll out and place in a 9-inch pie plate. Pierce with fork. Bake at 450 degrees F. for 7–9 minutes or until lightly browned. Cool.

2. For filling, spread enough jam to cover crust bottom.

3. Combine ricotta with egg yolks, sugar, vanilla, and butter. Stir in currants. Pour filling carefully over jam.

4. For topping, beat egg whites until foamy. Add sugar and beat until thickened.

5. Fold flour into whites. Fold whites into yolks. Place in pastry bag with large fluted end and squeeze lattice square designs over filling. Sprinkle with confectioners' sugar.

6. Bake at 350 degrees F. for 10 minutes or until lightly toasted. Remove from oven and place fresh blackberries between lattice work. Chill. Serves 6–8.

This pie takes less time than you may anticipate. The end result is impressive and tasty. You may vary the flavor of jam—strawberry, plum, even orange marmalade (but no watery jelly). In place of fresh fruit on top to correspond to the underlying jam, you may use teaspoon dabs of jams or marmalades.

Blueberry Apple Cheesecake

CRUST:
- 1 C unbleached all-purpose flour
- ½ t salt
- ⅓ C shortening
- 2 T white vinegar
- 2 T cold water

FILLING:
- 8 oz. cream cheese, softened
- 1 large egg
- ¾ C plus 2 T sugar, divided
- ½ t cinnamon
- 2 tart cooking apples sliced ¼-inch thick
- 2 C fresh blueberries, washed, dried
- ¾ t allspice
- 2 T unbleached all-purpose flour
- butter
- confectioners' sugar

1. For crust, mix flour and salt. Cut in shortening. Stir in vinegar and water one T at a time to form dough into ball. Roll out and place in bottom and 1½ inches up side of 8-inch springform pan. Pierce with fork. Bake at 450 degrees F. for 7–9 minutes or until lightly toasted.

2. For filling, beat cheese and egg together until smooth and light. Beat in 2 T sugar. Spread evenly on crust.

3. Sprinkle mixture of ¼ C sugar and cinnamon over apples. Place apple slices neatly in overlapping circles on cheese mixture.

4. Mix blueberries, ½ C sugar, allspice, and flour. Gently pour berries over apples. Dot with butter.

5. Bake at 400 degrees F. for 50–60 minutes or until done. Cool. Chill. Dust with confectioners' sugar. Serves 5–6.

Frozen blueberries may be used for this. If you pick your own to freeze, a handy way to store them is placing two cups in each bag. This way you know the measurements right away. Serve this dish with either a dusting of confectioners' sugar, a scoop of fresh homemade vanilla ice cream, or light cream streaming over the top and down the dark blueberries.

Blueberry Cheesecake I

CRUST:

1½ C graham cracker crumbs
1   t freshly ground nutmeg
2   T sugar
⅓   C sweet butter, melted

FILLING:

2   T unflavored gelatin
¼   C water
3   eggs, separated
1   C sugar
½   C milk
1   t vanilla extract
    dash of salt
2   C ricotta
1   C all-purpose cream

TOPPING:

1   T dark brown sugar
½   C graham cracker crumbs
¼   t cinnamon
    dash of nutmeg
2   T sweet butter, melted
1   C fresh blueberries

GLAZE:

1   C fresh blueberries
¼   C sugar
¼   C water
    dash of cinnamon

1. For crust, mix crumbs, nutmeg, sugar, and butter. Line bottom and side of an 8-inch springform pan. Bake at 450 degrees F. for 4 minutes or until set.
2. For filling, soften gelatin in water. Dissolve in top of double boiler over hot water. Set aside.
3. Combine egg yolks with sugar and milk. Add to gelatin mixture in double boiler. Cook slowly, stirring constantly, until thickened slightly.
4. Remove from heat. Stir in vanilla and salt. Cool.
5. Place ricotta into large bowl. Pour gelatin mixture into cheese and mix well. Refrigerate 20–30 minutes, stirring regularly.
6. Beat egg whites until stiff.
7. Whip cream until soft peaks form.
8. Fold egg whites and cream into the cheese mixture.
9. Pour filling into crust. Chill 2 hours or until set.
10. For topping, mix sugar, crumbs, cinnamon, nutmeg, and butter. Sprinkle over top of cake. Spread on whole blueberries.
11. For glaze (just before serving), combine 1 C blueberries, sugar, water, and cinnamon and bring to a boil. Crush berries while they're cooking. Simmer 5 minutes or until thickened. Cool slightly. Carefully pour over cake top or individual slices. Serves 8–10.

Wild blueberries that you pick yourself are smaller than the cultivated ones, but they're much more tasty and sweet, especially if picked at the height of a good sunny, rainy August. They freeze well. Just pick over clean berries (don't wash them until you're ready to use them later) and freeze. This recipe contains both whole berries and deep-colored blueberry syrup, two imperial but simple foods.

Blueberry Cheesecake II

2   T sweet butter, softened
2½ C blueberries
2   T unflavored gelatin
¾   C sugar
¼   t salt
1   egg yolk
¾   C milk
    grated rind of 1 fresh lemon
3   C cottage cheese, drained
2   t lemon juice
1   egg white
¾   C heavy cream
    confectioners' sugar

1. Spread butter around bottom and side of 1½ quart baking dish.
2. Stick a single layer of blueberries to the butter to form a shell of berries. Sprinkle with sugar.
3. Mix gelatin, sugar, salt, egg yolk, and milk in double boiler. Cook over hot water until slightly thickened. Add grated lemon rind. Cool.
4. Sieve and add cottage cheese and lemon juice.
5. Beat egg white until stiff. Fold into mixture.
6. Beat cream until stiff. Fold in.
7. Carefully pour cheese mixture into shell of berries. Chill. Garnish with blueberries. Dust with confectioners' sugar. Serves 6.

The blueberry season begins in May in North Carolina, and as the growing season moves north up the East Coast the season ends with berries ripening in September and early October in Maine and Nova Scotia. When taking out slices of this cake, use a spatula gingerly to better get the crust of berries.

Blueberry Cheesecake III

2	C unbleached all-purpose flour
¾	C granulated sugar
1½	t baking powder
½	t baking soda
½	t salt
¾	t freshly grated nutmeg
½	C grated sharp Cheddar cheese
½	C grated Swiss cheese
1	C blueberries
1	C orange juice
2	T sweet butter, melted, and butter for pan
1	large egg, slightly beaten

1. Combine flour, sugar, baking powder, baking soda, salt, nutmeg. Add cheeses and blueberries. Mix well.
2. Add juice, butter, and egg. Blend well.
3. Pour into buttered 8-inch springform pan. Bake at 350 degrees F. for 40–45 minutes or until center is set and top is golden. Serves 6–8.

More a familiar coffeecake, this delicious, easy-to-make dish is perfect for breakfast on a lazy Sunday. Slices are particularly tasty when served warm and with sweet butter on top. A simple vanilla confectioners' sugar icing is also good for this. If you use frozen blueberries, thaw and dry them first to reduce staining the dough as much as possible.

Blueberry Cheese Pie

CRUST:

1	C unbleached all-purpose flour
½	t salt
⅓	C shortening
3–4	T cold water

FILLING:

4	C blueberries, washed and drained
1	C water, divided
¾	C sugar
1	t cinnamon
2	T cornstarch
3	oz. cream cheese, softened

1. For crust, mix flour and salt. Cut in shortening. Stir in water one T at a time until dough forms a ball. Chill. Roll out for a 9-inch pie plate. Pierce with fork. Bake at 450 degrees F. for 7–9 minutes or until lightly toasted.

2. For filling, simmer 1 C berries and ⅔ C water for 3 minutes.

3. Blend sugar, cinnamon, cornstarch, and remaining ⅓ C water. Add to berries.

4. Boil ½ minute, stirring constantly. Cool.

5. Spread cheese over bottom of cooled crust.

6. Place 2½ C berries over cheese.

7. Cover with cooked mixture.

8. Garnish with ½ C berries.

9. Refrigerate 2 hours or until set. Serve with whipped cream. Serves 6.

Blueberries and huckleberries are often thought to be too close to separate. Actually, they come from two different plants and are distinguished clearly by their seeds. The blueberry (usually lighter in color) contains many tiny seeds, while the huckleberry has exactly ten larger seeds. Whether made from blue or huckle, this berry pie may be prepared in less than forty-five minutes. Top with fresh rich homemade vanilla ice cream for a first-rate treat.

Buttermilk Apricot Cheesecake

CRUST:
  1 C graham cracker crumbs
  ½ t coriander
  3½ T sweet butter, melted

FILLING:
  11 oz. dried apricots
  2 C buttermilk
  ½ C brown sugar
  ¾ t mace
  2 eggs, separated
  5 T sugar, divided
  8 oz. cream cheese, softened
  1 large egg
  ½ t vanilla extract

TOPPING:
  1 C sour cream
  2 T sugar
  ½ t vanilla extract

1. For crust, mix crumbs and coriander. Stir crumbs into melted butter and mix well. Press onto bottom and up side about 1½ inches of an 8-inch springform pan. Bake at 450 degrees F. for 4 minutes or until set. Cool.

2. For filling, simmer apricots in buttermilk 40–60 minutes until very soft, stirring occasionally. Remove from heat and mash very well to nearly a purée.

3. Stir in brown sugar (add more if less tartness is desired), mace, and egg yolks.

4. In separate bowl beat whites until soft peaks form, and add 2 T sugar. Continue beating until thickened. Fold into apricot mixture.

5. Beat cheese and egg until light. Beat in vanilla and 3 T sugar. Spread cheese mixture over crust.

6. Gently pour and spread apricot mixture over cheese. Bake at 325 degrees F. for 35–40 minutes or until lightly toasted.

7. For topping, mix sour cream, sugar, and vanilla. Remove cake from oven and gently spread on cream. Bake additional 7–9 minutes or until sour cream is set. Cool in pan. Remove side and chill for 2 hours. Serves 8–10.

You can make your own authentic buttermilk by buying fresh un-homogenized milk from a dairy. Then skim off the cream and churn it into butter (whirling it in a blender for 5–10 minutes is an easy way). The leftover liquid is the milk from the butter—buttermilk. Another way is to add a quarter to a half cup of commercial buttermilk to each quart of skim milk and set in a warm place until it clabbers. Most commercial buttermilk has butter fat added to it. Real buttermilk is easier to digest because the large butterfat solids are removed. This cake has a tangy flavor. The buttermilk may curdle slightly while simmering, but eventually the apricots absorb it. Be sure to mash the apricots thoroughly and well (a potato masher works). The thin white layers top and bottom make a nice border to the thick mellow orange filling.

Buttermilk Ricotta Pie

CRUST:

1½ C unbleached all-purpose
    flour
¾ t salt
3 T sweet butter
4 T shortening
3–4 T cold water

FILLING:

3 eggs, separated
¼ C sweet butter, melted
3 T unbleached all-purpose
    flour
¼ t salt
1 C sugar, divided
2 t vanilla extract
    grated rind of 1 fresh
    lemon
1½ C buttermilk
¾ C ricotta

SAUCE:

1 C water
⅓ C sugar
1 T cornstarch
3 T sweet butter
    grated rind of ½ fresh
    lemon
    juice of ½ fresh lemon

1. For crust, mix flour and salt. Cut in butter and shortening. Stir in water one T at a time to form dough into ball. Chill. Roll out and place in 10-inch pie plate. Pierce with fork. Bake at 450 degrees F. for 7–9 minutes or until lightly toasted. Cool.

2. For filling, beat egg yolks slightly and stir into cooled melted butter.

3. Combine flour, salt, and ½ C sugar. Mix into the egg yolk mixture.

4. Add vanilla, lemon rind, buttermilk, and ricotta.

5. Beat egg whites until soft peaks form. Continue to beat, gradually adding remaining ½ C sugar until meringue forms stiff peaks.

6. Carefully fold meringue into ricotta mixture. Pour into crust.

7. Bake at 350 degrees F. for 40 minutes or until center of pie is set and top is well toasted. Chill.

8. For sauce, mix water, sugar, and cornstarch and heat slowly in double boiler until thickened, stirring constantly with a whisk. Remove from heat and blend in butter, lemon rind, and juice. Drape warm or cold over pie wedges. Serves 6.

True ricotta is not the whole-milk variety found in supermarkets (although this is the next best to it) but is made from the whey left over when curd is formed into cheese. True ricotta is difficult to come by and is not really interchangeable with cottage cheese if you're after authentic ricotta taste. This is a light summery-tasting pie. The center sinks slightly, so a topping of sweetened fruit over the sauce might be a good idea.

Carrot Cognac Cheesecake

CRUST:

1	C graham cracker crumbs
1	t cinnamon
2	T sugar
¼	C sweet butter, melted

FILLING:

1	lb. cream cheese, softened
4	large eggs
¼	C unbleached all-purpose flour
⅞	C sugar
¼	C Cognac
½	t allspice
2	C cooked carrots, mashed
⅓	C plain yogurt

GLAZE:

2	T apricot jam
1½	T ground walnuts

1. For crust, mix crumbs, cinnamon, and sugar. Stir in butter and blend thoroughly. Press into bottom and up side of 8-inch springform pan. Bake at 450 degrees F. for 4 minutes or until set. Cool.

2. For filling, beat cheese, adding eggs one at a time.

3. Add flour, sugar, Cognac, and allspice. Beat in well.

4. Fold in mashed carrots. Fold in yogurt. Blend thoroughly.

5. Pour into crust. Bake at 325 degrees F. for 60–65 minutes or until lightly toasted. Turn off heat and open oven door slightly. After ½ hour remove cake and cool.

6. For glaze, heat jam and brush thick layer on top of cake. Sprinkle on walnuts. Chill for 2 hours. Serves 8–10.

Carrots have a surprising and untapped versatility. Young, sweet, tender carrots at the height of their garden freshness make the best ingredients, whether for carrot bread, cookies, cakes, puddings, or cheesecakes. For this recipe, boil the carrots thoroughly and then mash them thoroughly. The pulp blends easily with the cheese mixture and produces a cake that is softly colored both on top and inside. The carrot taste is nearly undetectable, but the effect is moist and mysteriously flavored.

Cassata alla Siciliana

1 8-inch spongecake

FILLING:
1½ lbs. ricotta
½ C sugar
1 t vanilla extract
2 oz. bitter chocolate, finely chopped

FROSTING:
1 egg white
1½ C confectioners' sugar
1 t almond extract
1 t fresh lemon juice
⅓ C candied fruits, chopped
⅓ C toasted almond slivers

1. Split cake into 3 layers.
2. Beat ricotta until smooth and light. Mix in sugar and vanilla. Fold in chocolate.
3. Spread half of filling on first layer. Stack second layer on filling. Repeat with remaining filling on second layer, placing third layer on top.
4. For frosting, beat egg white until soft peaks form. Beat in sugar, almond, and lemon juice until whites thicken.
5. Spread frosting over top and side of cake.
6. Sprinkle candied fruits on cake top.
7. Press almond slivers around the top edge of the cake. Chill. Serves 8–10.

The Sicilian cassata has many variations. Some incorporate the candied fruits into the ricotta filling along with the chocolate. Others don't frost the cake at all, relying on a sprinkle of confectioners' sugar instead. This version adds more formality to the cake, but still retains the gaiety of the citron and almonds. As for the chocolate, you might use semisweet by preference instead of the bitter.

Cheddar Apple Cheesecake

CAKE:

1½	C unbleached all-purpose flour
½	C whole wheat flour
½	C sugar
1½	t baking powder
1	t salt
¼	C sweet butter
1½	C shredded Cheddar cheese
1	large egg, slightly beaten
¾	C milk
3	large cooking apples, peeled, cored, sliced

GLAZE:

¾	C sugar
½	t cinnamon
⅓	C water
¼	C sweet butter
1	T lemon juice

1. For cake, mix together flours, sugar, baking powder, and salt.

2. Cut in butter until mixture resembles coarse meal.

3. Add cheese and blend lightly with flour mixture.

4. Combine egg and milk. Add to cheese mixture and blend.

5. Spread less than half of batter evenly in buttered and floured 9-inch square pan. Place apple slices over batter. Carefully spread on rest of batter. Place rest of apples decoratively on top.

6. Bake at 375 degrees F. for 35 minutes.

7. For glaze, blend sugar and cinnamon in saucepan. Add water, butter, lemon juice, and bring to boil.

8. Remove from heat and cool slightly.

9. Remove cake from oven. Pour glaze over cake.

10. Return cake to oven and bake 15 minutes more or until cake is well browned and apples are soft. Serves 9.

Few foods provide a more felicitous combination than Cheddar cheese and apples. Northern Spies, Greening, Winesap, and other tart cooking apples should be used for this dish. After you return the cake to the oven, watch toward the end of the time so that the glaze doesn't burn. This one is good warm.

Cheddar Cheesecake

1½ lbs. cream cheese, softened
5 eggs, separated
1 C sugar
1½ t vanilla extract
¼ C unbleached all-purpose
   flour
1 t fresh lemon juice
1 C sour cream
¾ C grated sharp Cheddar
   cheese
1 C all-purpose cream,
   whipped
   about a dozen fresh whole
   strawberries

1. Beat cream cheese with egg yolks until smooth and light.
2. Gradually mix in sugar, vanilla, and flour.
3. Beat in lemon juice and sour cream.
4. Add Cheddar.
5. Beat egg whites until stiff peaks form. Fold into cheese mixture.
6. Pour mixture into 9-inch springform pan.
7. Bake at 325 degrees F. for 1 hour or until center is set. Turn off heat and open oven door, leaving cake inside for ½ hour. Remove cake and cool.
8. Spread whipped cream on top and decorate with whole strawberries dipped in Kirsch. Serves 10–12.

Strawberries ripen in late spring and early summer. Justly one of the most popular berries, strawberries continue to be one of the largest berry harvests in the country. Picking your own at farms assures absolute freshness. Strawberries are said to have received their name from their having been taken to market strung on straws. The smaller berries are always less pulpy and more flavorful for this and other dishes.

Cheeseless Cheesecake

4 eggs, separated
15 oz. sweetened condensed
     milk
⅓ C lemon juice
1 t grated fresh lemon rind
1 t vanilla extract
½ t freshly ground nutmeg
⅔ C Zwieback crumbs
2 T sugar
2 T sweet butter, melted

1. Beat egg yolks and milk together.
2. Add lemon juice, rind, vanilla, and nutmeg.
3. In separate bowl beat egg whites until stiff peaks form. Fold into milk mixture.
4. Mix crumbs, sugar, and butter. Sprinkle half of crumb mixture over the bottom of a buttered 9-inch square pan.
5. Pour in milk mixture. Sprinkle remaining crumbs on top.
6. Bake at 325 degrees F. for 30 minutes. Cool 1 hour in oven with the door closed. Serves 9.

This dish is a contradiction in terms and a gimmick, but it's a good mock cheesecake that's fast to make. The reaction of the yolks, milk, and lemon juice works to thicken fairly quickly, so work fast.

Cherry Cheese Pie

CRUST:

1   C unbleached all-purpose
    flour
½   t salt
3   T sweet butter
3   T shortening
3–4 T cold water

FILLING:

8   oz. cream cheese, softened
⅓   C sugar
1   T unbleached all-purpose
    flour
2   eggs, beaten well
¼   t vanilla extract
¼   t almond extract
¼   C sour cream

GLAZE:

3   T sugar
1   T cornstarch
¼   t mace
1   lb. jar pitted sour cherries,
    juice reserved

1. For crust, mix flour and salt. Cut in butter and shortening. Stir in water one T at a time to form dough into ball. Chill. Roll out and place into a 9-inch pie plate. Pierce with fork. Bake at 450 degrees F. for 7–9 minutes or until lightly toasted.

2. For filling, combine cream cheese, sugar, and flour. Add eggs, vanilla and almond extracts, and sour cream. Blend well.

3. Pour into crust and bake at 350 degrees F. for 20 minutes or until center is set. Cool.

4. For glaze, combine sugar, cornstarch, and mace. Slowly stir in 1 C cherry juice (add water if needed) into sugar mixture. Cook over low heat, stirring, until mixture thickens and turns transparent.

5. Place cherries on top of pie.

6. Pour glaze over cherries. Chill. Serves 6.

While sweet cherries are usually reserved for eating fresh, sour cherries are the cook's delight. They add a velvety texture and smooth taste, as they do for this pie. At first the cornstarch in the glaze seems to cloud the deep rich color of the juice, but as it cooks it thins and disappears. You'll get rid of any residue cornstarchy taste if you continue to simmer the syrup for five minutes or so.

Cherry Clafouti Cheesecake

CAKE:
1 17-oz. jar dark sweet
   cherries, drained and
   pitted (reserve juice)
½ C unbleached all-purpose
   flour
2 t baking powder
   dash of salt
1 t cinnamon
3 large eggs, separated
8 oz. cream cheese, softened
½ C milk
⅓ C sugar, divided
   confectioners' sugar

SAUCE:
   reserved cherry juice
¼ C red wine
2 t cornstarch dissolved in 2 t
   water

1. For cake, drain and pit cherries. Set juice aside.
2. Mix flour, baking powder, salt, cinnamon.
3. Beat yolks and cheese together. Stir in milk and 3 T sugar.

4. Whip whites until frothy. Beat in remaining sugar until dissolved and whites have thickened.
5. Combine flour and cheese mixtures.
6. Fold whites into mixture.
7. Spread half of batter on bottom of buttered 8-inch springform pan. Place half of cherries evenly spaced over batter. Spread on rest of batter and then remainder of cherries.
8. Bake at 350 degrees F. for 30–40 minutes or until top is golden brown. Cool on wire rack before removing pan. Dust rim edge of cake with confectioners' sugar.
9. For sauce, combine cherry juice with wine in saucepan. In separate cup, dissolve cornstarch in water. Stir into juice and heat slowly to thicken. Boil gently for about 4–5 minutes. Pour sauce over individual wedges. Serves 6.

You can easily pit the cherries without damaging their shape too much by forcing the seed out the stem end. If you don't have a shaker, an easy way to dust on the confectioners' sugar is to stir the end of a wooden spoon in a fine-meshed tea strainer containing the sugar. This variation of a favorite provincial French dessert is delicate, not cheesy, not overly sweet or rich. Drape the sauce over the middle section of the wedges for a colorful display. Serve the cake at room temperature.

Chocolate Cheese Pie I

CRUST:

1   C graham cracker crumbs
3   T cocoa
2   T sugar
¼   C sweet butter, melted

FILLING:

6   oz. semisweet chocolate bits
¾   C dark brown sugar, divided
8   oz. cream cheese, softened
    dash of salt
1   t vanilla extract
2   large eggs, separated
1   C all-purpose cream,
    whipped

1. For crust, mix crumbs, cocoa, and sugar. Stir in butter and blend thoroughly. Pat crumbs into a 9-inch pie plate. Bake at 450 degrees F. for 4 minutes or until set. Cool.

2. For filling, melt chocolate over simmering water in double boiler. Cool slightly.
3. Cream ½ C brown sugar, cheese, salt, and vanilla.
4. Beat in egg yolks, one at a time.
5. Beat in cooled chocolate. Blend thoroughly.
6. In separate bowl beat egg whites until stiff but not dry.
7. Gradually add ¼ C brown sugar to the whites, beating until stiff and glossy.
8. Fold whites into chocolate mixture. Fold in whipped cream.
9. Set aside ¼ of the mixture for garnish. Pour the rest into the crust.
10. Refrigerate until filling sets. With large spoon, drop reserved mixture in mounds over top of pie.
11. Refrigerate overnight. Serves 6–9.

Like the coffee bean, the cacao bean is dried and roasted to start the elaborate process that allows it to take on its singular flavor. Each pod from the cacao tree contains up to forty seeds. After some of the cocoa butter is removed, the bean is crushed to yield cocoa powder. Ever since Aztec King Montezuma II offered Cortez a golden cup of chocolate in the sixteenth century, chocolate has been one of the most treasured tastes of the world. Nothing takes its place, including carob. Good authentic chocolate should never be taken for granted.

Chocolate Cheese Pie II

CRUST:
- 1 C unbleached all-purpose flour
- ½ t salt
- ⅓ C shortening
- 3–4 T cold water

FILLING:
- 1 T unflavored gelatin
- ¼ C cold water
- 1 oz. unsweetened chocolate
- 1 C hot water
- ⅔ C sugar
- ½ t vanilla extract
- dash of salt
- 8 oz. cream cheese, softened
- ½ C all-purpose cream, whipped

1. For crust, mix flour and salt. Cut in shortening. Add water one T at a time to form dough into a ball. Roll out and place in a 9-inch pie plate. Pierce with fork. Bake at 450 degrees F. for 7–9 minutes or until lightly toasted. Cool.

2. For filling, sprinkle gelatin over cold water to soften in a mixing bowl.

3. Melt chocolate over simmering water in double boiler and gradually stir in hot water. Continue heating until blended.

4. Add sugar, vanilla, and salt to gelatin and stir well. Combine with chocolate.

5. In separate bowl beat cream cheese until smooth and light. Add chocolate-gelatin mixture and blend. Refrigerate until slightly thickened.

6. Fold whipped cream into cheese mixture. Pour into crust.

7. Chill until firm. Garnish with whipped cream and grated sweet chocolate. Serves 6–8.

This eggless cheese pie relies on the gelatin to turn it firm. Since chocolate tends to burn fairly easily (even chocolate cakes should be baked at slightly lower temperatures than you'd use for other cakes), it's wise to melt it slowly in a double boiler. However, you can melt chocolate squares directly over electric burners if you use a heavy saucepan, keep the burner at the lowest possible setting, and watch the chocolate continuously.

Chocolate Coffee Rum Cheesecake

24   chocolate wafers
5   T sweet butter, melted

FILLING:
1   lb. cream cheese, softened
⅞   C sugar
3   large eggs, separated
2   t instant espresso coffee
     powder
1   oz. unsweetened chocolate,
     melted
¼   C dark rum
¼   C unbleached all-purpose
     flour
¼   t salt
⅓   C heavy cream, whipped
2   T toasted blanched almonds,
     finely ground

1. For crust, grind wafers to crumbs. Mix in butter. Press crumbs onto bottom and up 1½ inches of side of 8-inch springform pan. Bake at 450 degrees F. for 4 minutes or until set. Chill.

2. For filling, beat cheese, sugar, egg yolks, coffee, chocolate, rum, and flour together until smooth and light.

3. In separate bowl beat egg whites and salt until stiff peaks form. Fold into cheese mixture.

4. Pour mixture into prepared crust. Bake 35 minutes at 350 degrees F. or until center is set.

5. Keep in oven with door partially open for 30 minutes more. Remove from oven and cool. Remove the side of the pan and chill.

6. Spread whipped cream ¾ of an inch thick on center top of cake, leaving an inch of the raised edge of the cake visible.

7. Sprinkle ground almonds over whipped cream. Serves 6–8.

The black wafer crust circling the mocha rim of the cake, topped by a ring of white cream sprinkled with the ocher ground almonds, entices your eyes as much as the rich creamy texture does your tastebuds. Don't worry if the center of the cake splits as it bakes; the whipped cream will conceal the cracks. If you start with whole almonds, simply boil a few for a minute or two, remove the skins, and toast them slowly (so the insides dry) in an iron skillet. Then whirl them in a blender to a powder. For a fine, even sprinkle on the cake, shake the almond powder through a sieve over the whipped cream.

Chocolate Honey Cheesecake

CAKE:

1½ C unbleached all-purpose
    flour
½   C sugar
1   t baking soda
½   t salt
8   oz. cream cheese, softened
2   large eggs
3   oz. unsweetened chocolate
¼   C sweet butter, melted
½   C honey
1   t vanilla extract
½   C buttermilk
½   C strong espresso coffee

ICING:

3   T sweet butter
3   T cocoa
1   T honey
½   t vanilla extract
1   C confectioners' sugar
1   T milk

1. For cake, mix flour, sugar, soda, and salt. Set aside.
2. In large mixing bowl beat cheese and eggs together until very light and smooth.
3. In separate saucepan melt chocolate over simmering water. Combine butter and chocolate.
4. Add honey and vanilla to chocolate mixture. Blend.
5. Combine buttermilk and coffee.
6. Pour chocolate mixture into cheese mixture. Blend well.
7. Gradually alternate stirring buttermilk and flour mixtures into the cheese mixture. Blend well.
8. Pour batter into a buttered 12 × 8 × 2-inch baking dish. Bake at 325 degrees F. for 25–30 minutes (do not overbake). Cool in dish on rack.
9. For icing, cream butter, cocoa, honey, and vanilla. Add sugar and milk and beat well. Spread on cooled cake. Serves 8–10.

Moist, dark, rich, and beyond merely delicious, this is the kind of chocolate cake that you savor with a tall clear glass of cold milk. It also illustrates the fact that cream cheese may be effectively used to produce cheesecakes far and wide of the familiar ones. Any number of icings may be used on this—fluffy white, orange, mocha—but a straightforward one, as suggested here, seems to better underscore the specialness of the cake itself.

Chocolate Malt Cheesecake

CRUST:

1 C graham cracker crumbs
¼ C sweet butter, melted

FILLING:

1 lb. cream cheese, softened
2 large eggs, separated
¼ C unbleached all-purpose
    flour
1 t vanilla extract
¼ C all-purpose cream
½ C sugar, divided
⅓ C instant chocolate malt mix

1. For crust, mix crumbs and melted butter. Press into 8-inch springform pan to make thin bottom and side layers. Bake at 450 degrees F. for 4 minutes or until set. Cool.

2. For filling, beat cheese, egg yolks, flour, vanilla, and cream until smooth and light.

3. Stir in ¼ C sugar and malt. Beat until well blended.

4. Beat egg whites until soft peaks form. Add ¼ C sugar and beat until stiff and glossy.

5. Fold whites into the cheese mixture. Pour into prepared crust.

6. Bake at 325 degrees F. for 30 minutes or until center is set (don't overbake, or large cracks will form).

7. Remove from oven and cool to room temperature before removing pan side. Chill before serving. Serves 6.

A creamy texture, together with the tan color and moderate size, make this a good one for a midday snack. Although prepared with cream cheese, it's not heavy—but rich, it is. The shy malt taste turns this cake just oblique enough to spark interest. Besides all this, the cake is relatively quick and straightforward to make for the rewards of a slightly different cheesecake taste.

Cocoa Cheesecake

FILLING:
1   C cottage cheese, drained, sieved
¼   C sugar
1   large egg, well beaten
1   T cornstarch
¼   t salt
1   t vanilla extract
½   t cinnamon

BATTER:
1   C unbleached all-purpose flour
⅔   C sugar
½   C cocoa
¾   t baking powder
¼   t salt
¼   C sweet butter, melted, and butter for pan
2   large eggs
¼   C milk
1   t vanilla extract

1. For filling, mix cottage cheese, sugar, egg, cornstarch, salt, vanilla, and cinnamon. Set aside.
2. For batter, blend flour, sugar, cocoa, baking powder, and salt.
3. Combine butter, eggs, milk, and vanilla.
4. Combine butter and flour mixtures and beat for 3 minutes.
5. Spread half of this batter in a buttered 8-inch-square pan.
6. Pour cottage cheese mixture on top. Spread on remaining batter.
7. Bake at 350 degrees F. for 40 minutes or until center is set. Cool in pan on rack. Serves 6–9.

This basic coffeecake-like dish has a surprisingly moist center. It's good as a change from the standard baking-powder–brown-sugar-cinnamon cake for Sunday morning breakfast. Like the latter, this is good served warm.

Cocoa Cheese Pie

CRUST:
- 1 C graham cracker crumbs
- 2 T sugar
- ¼ C sweet butter, melted

FILLING:
- 12 oz. cream cheese, softened
- ¾ C sugar
- ¼ C cocoa
- 1 t vanilla extract
- 2 large eggs

TOPPING:
- 1 C sour cream
- 2 T sugar
- 1 t vanilla extract

1. For crust, mix crumbs and sugar. Stir in butter and mix well. Press into 9-inch pie plate. Reserve 2 T for garnish. Bake at 450 degrees F. for 4 minutes or until set. Cool.

2. For filling, blend cheese, sugar, cocoa, and vanilla. Beat in eggs one at a time.

3. Pour into crust and bake at 375 degrees F. for 25 minutes or until center is set. Remove from oven and cool slightly.

4. For topping, combine sour cream, sugar, and vanilla. Spread over pie. Sprinkle on reserved crumbs.

5. Return pie to oven for 8–10 minutes or until sour cream sets. Cool. Chill. Serves 6.

This is a hurry-up pie that is easy to prepare and good to serve. The sour cream white topping keeps the cocoa-colored, cocoa-tasting filling a surprise until the pie is cut. Don't overbake the sour cream when you return the pie to the oven, or the top will crack.

Coeurs à la Crème I
(cream hearts)

8 oz. cream cheese, softened
½ t vanilla extract
½ C confectioners' sugar
1 C heavy cream
   cheesecloth
   strawberries

1. Beat cheese until very smooth and light. Add vanilla. Slowly add sugar while beating until well mixed.
2. In separate bowl beat the cream until stiff peaks form. Fold into cheese mixture.
3. Line six 3-inch coeurs à la crème molds with wet and wrung cheesecloth sections, leaving enough cloth to overhang the molds.
4. Spoon the mixture into the molds and pack it down firmly. Fold over the cheesecloth and chill overnight.
5. To serve, unfold cheesecloth. Invert mold on plate. Lift off the mold from the cheesecloth. Then carefully peel off the cheesecloth. Encircle the coeurs à la crème with small ripe strawberries dipped in dry red wine. Serves 6.

Also known as heart's delight, these simple cheesecakes have been elevated from peasant farm kitchens to sophisticated dinner desserts. They may also be served nicely with strawberry or raspberry sauce draped over them slightly.

Coeur à la Crème II

8 oz. cream cheese, softened
1 C cottage cheese, drained,
    sieved
¼ C confectioners' sugar
1 C heavy cream
    cheesecloth

SAUCE:
1½ pints fresh strawberries, 10
    reserved
¼ C sugar
2 T dry red wine

1. Beat cream cheese until smooth and light.
2. In separate bowl beat cottage cheese until smooth.
3. Combine cheeses. Add sugar and beat until light.
4. In separate bowl beat cream until stiff peaks form. Fold into cheese mixture.
5. Line a 3-cup mold with wet and wrung cheesecloth, leaving enough cloth to overhang the mold.
6. Place mixture into mold, pack down firmly, and fold cheesecloth over cheese. Chill a full day or overnight.
7. To serve, unfold cheesecloth. Invert mold onto plate. Carefully lift off mold from cheesecloth. Then peel cloth gently away from cheese.
8. For sauce, whirl the prepared strawberries in a blender. Stir in sugar and wine. Chill.
9. Dip bottom half of small fresh ripe strawberries in confectioners' sugar and arrange them around the coeur à la crème, placing one or two decoratively on top of the mold. Drape sauce decoratively over mold or individual servings. Serves 8.

Variations of the coeur à la crème may be made with ricotta instead of the cottage cheese, or substituting one-half cup of sour cream for one-half cup of the heavy cream. The cheese may be molded in any shape or appropriate size, but the traditional form is a small or—as is this case—large heart mold.

Coffee Cheese Pie

CRUST:

1½ C graham cracker crumbs
¼   C dark brown sugar
½   t cinnamon
¾   C cocoa
⅓   C sweet butter, melted

FILLING:

1   T unflavored gelatin
½   C water
½   t instant espresso coffee
     mix
14   oz. sweetened condensed
     milk
1½   t vanilla extract
1   lb. cream cheese, softened
1   C all-purpose cream,
     whipped
¼   C sliced almonds

1. For crust, mix crumbs, sugar, cinnamon, and cocoa. Stir in butter. Press into 10-inch pie plate. Bake at 450 degrees F. for 4 minutes or until set. Cool.

2. For filling, soften gelatin in ¼ C cold water in saucepan. Add coffee mix. Place over medium-low heat, stirring constantly until dissolved. Remove from heat.

3. Blend in milk and vanilla.

4. Beat cheese until smooth and light. Beat in cocoa mixture.

5. Fold in whipped cream. Pour into crust. Sprinkle on the almonds decoratively. Refrigerate until set and chilled, about 2 hours. Serves 6–8.

Once again the felicitous combination of coffee and chocolate. This rendition is creamy and smooth. It makes a high and wide sumptuous slice to end a meal. A little Cognac to top it all off is perfect.

Coffee Rum Cheese Pie

CRUST:

1¼ C unbleached all-purpose
     flour
¾ t salt
3 T sweet butter
3 T shortening
4 T cold water

FILLING:

12 oz. cream cheese, softened
1 C sugar
3 T very strong espresso
    coffee
2 T dark rum
    grated rind of 1 fresh lemon
1 T unflavored gelatin
    dissolved in 2 T hot water
1 C all-purpose cream

1. For crust, mix flour and salt. Cut in butter and shortening. Stir in water one T at a time until dough forms a ball. Roll out and place in a 9-inch pie plate. Pierce with fork. Bake at 450 degrees F. for 8–10 minutes or until lightly toasted. Cool.

2. For filling, beat cheese until smooth and light.

3. Beat in sugar. Add coffee, rum, and lemon peel, and mix well.

4. Dissolve gelatin in water. Blend in ½ C cheese mixture with gelatin and return it to the rest of the mixture. Stir well.

5. Whip cream until stiff peaks form. Fold into cheese mixture.

6. Pour into crust and refrigerate for 2 hours or until set. Serves 6–8.

Whether you're using a quart or three tablespoons of coffee, as in this recipe, it should be prepared fresh. Boiled coffee (or reheated coffee) is spoiled coffee, as the old saying goes. The reason is that coffee fats melt into the brew the second time they're heated. Fresh coffee in this dish helps make the pie the way it should be—light, aromatic, and earthy tasting.

Cranberry Cherry Cheese Tart

CRUST:
1½   C unbleached all-purpose
       flour
¾   t salt
½   C shortening
4   T cold water

FILLING:
1½   C fresh cranberries
½   C water
¾   C sugar
1   T cornstarch dissolved in 1
       T water
8   oz. cream cheese, softened
2   large eggs
½   C sugar
1   T Kirsch
17   oz. dark sweet cherries,
       drained, pitted, halved

1. For crust, mix flour and salt. Cut in shortening. Stir in water one T at a time until dough forms a ball. Roll out only enough for bottom and side crust. Set rest aside (about ⅓ of the dough) for the lattice top. Place in 9-inch tart pan.
2. For filling, place cranberries, water, and sugar in saucepan. Bring to boil and then, stirring occasionally, cook over medium-low heat until berries burst.
3. Mix cornstarch with water and stir into cranberries. Continue cooking and stirring occasionally until slightly thickened.
4. Beat cheese until smooth and light. Add eggs, sugar, and Kirsch and beat well until slightly thickened.
5. Place cherries rounded side up over entire bottom crust.
6. Pour cheese mixture over cherries.
7. Carefully spoon cranberry mixture over cheese mixture, but do not cover completely. Leave some cheese exposed.
8. Roll out rest of dough and cut into long narrow (about ¼-inch wide) strips for the lattice. Place 11 strips across top of tart. Then place 9 strips diagonally (not at right angles) across the first strips. Pinch against side crust.
9. Bake at 325 degrees F. for 1 hour or until the crust is lightly toasted. Cool. Serves 6.

The dark sweet Black Tartarian cherries in a jar come ready to use for this recipe. This combination builds, rather than contrasts, the tartish taste of cranberries with the cherries, making a pleasant, subtle complement. The filling rises as it cooks, but will settle on cooling. Nevertheless, don't overfill the crust. This is a difficult tart to identify on sight, and for this reason it adds a playful and appropriate dessert around the fall holiday season.

Cranberry Currant Cheesecake

CRUST:
- 1 C cornflake crumbs
- 3 T sugar
- 1 t orange rind
- ¼ C sweet butter, melted

FILLING:
- 2 lbs. cottage cheese
- 4 large eggs
- ½ C all-purpose cream
- ¼ C unbleached all-purpose flour
- 2 C sugar, divided
- 1 T fresh lemon juice
- 2 t vanilla extract
- 2 C cranberries
- ⅓ C currants
- 1¼ C water, divided
- 1 T unflavored gelatin

1. For crust, mix crumbs with sugar and orange rind. Stir in butter. Press onto bottom and side of 9-inch springform pan. Bake at 450 degrees F. for 4 minutes or until set. Cool.

2. For filling, whirl half of cheese in a blender until smooth; repeat for the rest.

3. With electric mixer, beat together cheese, eggs, cream, flour, 1 C sugar, lemon juice, and vanilla. Pour into crust.

4. Bake at 350 degrees F. for 50 minutes. Turn off heat but keep cake inside oven for a half hour more. Remove from oven and cool. Then refrigerate for 2 hours.

5. Combine cranberries, currants, 1 C sugar, 1 C water. Stirring constantly, cook over medium-high heat until the berry skins pop.

6. Soften gelatin in ¼ C cold water. Stir well into cranberry mixture. Remove from heat. Refrigerate until thickened; stir occasionally.

7. Remove side of pan and place cake on serving platter. Spread cranberry mixture over top and drape some over side. Refrigerate another 2 hours. Serves 10–12.

Known originally as a crane berry on Cape Cod, Massachusetts, the cranberry exudes a tartness that is just right for the edge of fall and winter, when the small round red berry comes of age. Cranberry sauce and Thanksgiving dinner are inseparable. So this cranberry-currant topped cake makes an appropriate dish to herald in the tart frosty season of November and December.

Cranberry Orange Cheesecake

CRUST:
1   C unbleached all-purpose
    flour
½   t salt
¼   C sweet butter

FILLING:
6   oz. cranorange juice
    concentrate, thawed
2   large eggs
1   lb. cream cheese, softened
½   C sugar
¼   C unbleached all-purpose
    flour
¼   C heavy cream

1. For crust, mix flour and salt. Cut in butter. Place in 8-inch springform pan. Pat dough firmly on bottom and up side about 1½ inches.
2. For filling, place juice concentrate and eggs in a blender. Whirl briefly.
3. Add pieces of half the cheese and whirl until smooth. Repeat with rest of cheese.
4. Add sugar, flour, and cream and whirl until smooth and well blended.
5. Pour into crust and bake at 325 degrees F. for about 1 hour or until center is set. Keeping cake inside oven, turn off heat and half open door for about a half hour. Remove from oven. Cool before serving. Serves 6–8.

The pastel pink is as delicate as the subtle cranberry taste. The center sinks in the traditional cheesecake form, and the top browns slightly. This is a moist cake, easy to make, and enough of a detour from the familiar lemon cheesecake to make it appealing.

Crème de Menthe Cheesecake

CRUST:
- ⅓ C sweet butter
- ⅓ C honey
- 1 large egg
- 1¼ C unbleached all-purpose flour
- 2 T cocoa

FILLING:
- ¼ C unbleached all-purpose flour
- 1½ lbs. cream cheese, softened
- ½ C honey
- 4 large eggs
- ½ C green Crème de Menthe heavy cream, whipped, sweetened

1. For crust, cream butter and honey. Beat in egg. Stir in flour and cocoa. Press a thin layer onto bottom and side of 9-inch springform pan. Bake at 450 degrees F. for 8–10 minutes or until set. Cool.

2. For filling, cream flour, cream cheese, and honey.

3. Beat in eggs one at a time.

4. Blend in liqueur.

5. Pour into crust. Bake at 350 degrees F. for 45 minutes or until center is set. Cool. Chill. Top slices with dollops of sweetened whipped cream. Serves 10–12.

Being so sweet, liqueurs are properly served after dinner to stop the appetite. So it's fitting that a liqueur in a cheesecake, also an appetite-stopper, works well, as in this case. Crème de Menthe is made with strong mint flavor. In using honey in this recipe, you might coat your measuring cup with a thin layer of oil first. Then the honey will quickly slip out of the cup with none wasted.

Currant Cognac Cheesecake

CRUST:
1¼ C graham cracker crumbs
¼ C sweet butter, melted

FILLING:
⅓ C currants
⅓ C Cognac
8 oz. ricotta
8 oz. cream cheese, softened
3 T unbleached all-purpose flour
3 large eggs, beaten well
⅔ C sugar
 rind and juice of 1 lime
1 C heavy cream, whipped slightly

1. For crust, mix crumbs and butter well. Press into bottom and up side of an 8-inch springform pan. Bake at 450 degrees F. for 4 minutes or until set. Cool.

2. For filling, plump currants in Cognac for ½ hour. Drain off rest of Cognac, reserving 2 T.

3. Beat ricotta, cheese, and 2 T Cognac until smooth and light.

4. Beat in flour and eggs well. Beat in sugar and lime.

5. Fold in cream. Pour into crust.

6. Bake at 325 degrees F. for 50–60 minutes or until center is set. Open oven door slightly and turn off heat, allowing the cake to remain inside for ½ hour. Cool in pan. Chill. Serves 6–8.

Dried black or Zante currants plump with Cognac make a pleasant counterpoint taste when the currants are spread throughout the cake. Corinth (Greece) and California supply us with most of the currants (the word currant is a modification of *Corinth*). This is a moderately moist cake. The ricotta provides a lightness, the cream cheese a sturdiness.

Darioles

CRUST:
- 1 C unbleached all-purpose flour
- ½ t salt
- ⅓ C shortening
- 4 T cold water

FILLING:
- 3 oz. cream cheese, softened
- ¼ C light cream
- 2 large eggs
- ½ C sugar
- ½ C warm milk
- 2 t gelatin
- ½ t vanilla extract
- ½ C heavy cream, whipped
- ⅓ C toasted slivered almonds

1. For crust, mix flour and salt. Cut in shortening. Stir in water one T at a time until dough forms a ball. Roll out to ⅛-inch thickness. Place individual muffin tin open-side down on dough. With sharp knife cut a circle of dough around and about 1 inch wider than the rim. Take dough circle and place over bottom of tin, again open-side down. Pinch to make four corners. Press side of dough to the tin. If necessary, trim dough so that it is symmetrical around the tin. Pierce with fork. Bake at 450 degrees F. for about 7 minutes or until lightly toasted. Cool.

2. For filling, blend cheese and cream.

3. Beat eggs and sugar together in double boiler over simmering water.

4. Add milk, stirring constantly until mixture thickens. Remove from heat.

5. Soften gelatin in 1 T cold water. Add to milk mixture. Stir in vanilla. Cool.

6. Combine milk and cheese mixtures.

7. Fold in whipped cream.

8. Pour into crusts. Sprinkle on almonds. Chill. Makes 10–12.

Darioles are the medieval precursors of the modern-day cheesecakes. It's a lot easier, however, to use gelatin from an envelope rather than boiling pig hooves for thickeners. Dariole tins are marketed. They're large muffin cups; fluted tart pans work well, too.

Date Cheese Pie

CRUST:

1¼ C graham cracker crumbs
½   t cinnamon
2   T sugar
⅓   C sweet butter, melted

FILLING:

8   oz. cream cheese, softened
1   C cottage cheese
2   large eggs, beaten well
⅓   C sugar
¼   C sour cream
2   T unbleached all-purpose
    flour
1   t grated fresh lemon peel
1   T lemon juice
1   C chopped Medjools dates
¼   C chopped walnuts

1. For crust, mix crumbs, cinnamon, and sugar. Stir in butter. Press into 9-inch pie plate. Bake at 450 degrees F. for 4 minutes or until set. Cool.
2. For filling, beat cheeses until smooth and light.
3. Add eggs, beating until well blended.
4. Add sugar, cream, flour, lemon peel, and juice. Blend thoroughly.
5. Fold in dates.
6. Pour into cooled baked crust. Sprinkle with walnuts.
7. Bake at 300 degrees F. for 1 hour or until center is set. Cool. Serves 6.

Few people except date farmers realize the extraordinary care and work that goes into producing choice dates, the kind that are whole, soft, and irresistibly delicious. Select dates must be picked every day, at the height of their natural curing process, from the high date palm trees which must be carefully tended during the rest of the growing season. The culture of choice dates has been likened to the preparation of choice chocolates. The natural sugar content in dates reaches 65 percent. In this recipe it is best not to chop the dates too finely, or their luscious taste will be less appreciated.

Date Walnut Cheese Tart

CRUST:
¾ C unbleached all-purpose
    flour
¼ C walnut crumbs
½ t salt
¼ C shortening
1   egg yolk
    cold water as needed

FILLING:
8   oz. cream cheese, softened
½ C sour cream
½ C sugar
2   large eggs, slightly beaten
2   T almond-flavored liqueur
¾ C Medjools dates
¼ C walnut halves

GLAZE:
1   T apricot jam
1   t water

1. For crust, mix flour, walnut crumbs, and salt. Cut in shortening. Stir in egg yolk. Stir in water 1 T at a time until dough forms a ball. Roll out and place in a 9-inch tart pan. Pierce with fork. Bake at 450 degrees F. for 5–7 minutes or until lightly toasted. Cool.

2. For filling, beat cheese until smooth and light.

3. Blend in sour cream and sugar.

4. Beat in eggs. Stir in liqueur. Pour into crust.

5. Cut dates in half, removing pit. In circles, gently place dates and walnut halves alternately over entire filling.

6. Bake at 325 degrees F. for 30 minutes or until center of filling is set. Cool.

7. For glaze, heat jam and water together, stirring. Brush on cake. Chill. Serves 6–8.

This tart takes its origin from the wonderful combination of choice dates stuffed with walnuts or cream cheese. The American date crop is located in the southern desert, mostly in California. This is a rich, sweet tart, so a thin slice goes a long way.

Diet-Light Cheesecake

    sweet butter
½ C graham cracker crumbs

FILLING:
1 lb. ricotta
2 T sweet butter, melted
½ t salt
½ C unbleached all-purpose
     flour
    rind and juice of 1 lemon
1 large egg
⅔ C dry instant skim milk
1 t vanilla extract
6 egg whites
    pinch of fresh cream of tartar
⅔ C sugar
3 T water

1. For crust, butter the bottom and side of a 9-inch springform pan. Sprinkle on crumbs.

2. For filling, combine ricotta, butter, salt, flour, lemon rind and juice, and egg.

3. Stir in milk and vanilla.

4. Beat egg whites and cream of tartar until stiff.

5. In small heavy saucepan dissolve sugar into the water. Stirring constantly, boil 5 minutes until thickened.

6. Slowly pour hot syrup into whites and beat until stiff.

7. Fold the egg whites into the cheese mixture.

8. Pour into pan. Bake at 350 degrees F. for 40 minutes or until center is set. Turn off heat and keep cake in oven for another hour. Cool. Serves 6–8.

This light-textured cake is also light on the calories. Ricotta is a light cheese, six calorie-heavy egg yolks are *not* used, the dry milk has nearly all the fat removed, and sugar is kept to a minimum. A good wind-up to a light luncheon.

Dobos Cheesecake

6   large eggs, separated
1   C sugar
2   T dark rum
¾   C cake flour
¼   C cornstarch
    dash of salt
    sweet butter for pan

FILLING:
2   C ricotta
½   C sour cream
⅔   C confectioners' sugar
    grated rind of 1 lemon

GLAZE:
½   C apricot jam
    water

1. Beat egg yolks until light and lemon colored.
2. Gradually beat in sugar until dissolved. Stir in rum.
3. Beat egg whites until stiff. Set aside.
4. Mix flour, cornstarch, and salt.
5. Alternately fold egg whites and flour into yolk mixture, ending with whites.
6. In buttered 8-inch springform pan, spread ⅙ of batter evenly. Bake at 450 degrees F. for 4 minutes or until lightly toasted. Remove this thin cake layer from pan and cool. Repeat to make 5 similar layers.
7. For filling, combine ricotta, sour cream, confectioners' sugar, and lemon rind.
8. To assemble, place one cake layer on platter. Place ⅕ of the filling on layer. Repeat with other layers, ending with most attractively cooked layer.
9. For glaze, heat jam and only enough water to thin slightly. Pour jam over entire top of cake and allow it to fall over the side. Chill for 1–2 hours. Serves 8–10.

This variation of the multilayered chocolate-coated Dobos cake is not as rich as the original, but it's equally as eye-stopping. It stands about four inches high and, with the golden glaze and thin yellow layers and white cheese filling alternating up a ladder, the cake is very alluring. Since the layers cook very fast, it's not too time consuming. You can cut the recipe in half and still have a tempting dish. Also, thinned strawberry jam covering the top and side creates a different bright-flowered effect.

Dried Fruit Cheesecake

CRUST:

1 C graham cracker crumbs
1 T sugar
  dash of salt
¼ C sweet butter, melted

FILLING:

10 oz. dried fruit (8 apricots, 8
   prunes, 8 apples)
2 C water
8 oz. cream cheese, softened
1 C cottage cheese
2 large eggs
2 T lemon juice
¼ C sugar

GLAZE:

  reserved juice (about ⅓ C)
1 T honey
1 T corn syrup
1 T cornstarch dissolved in 1
  T water

1. For crust, mix crumbs, sugar, and salt. Stir in butter. Press onto bottom and up side of an 8-inch springform pan. Bake at 450 degrees F. for 4 minutes or until set. Cool.

2. For filling, cook fruit in water until very tender (about 15–20 minutes). Drain and reserve juice for glaze.

3. In blender whirl until smooth the cheeses, eggs, lemon juice, and sugar.

4. Place half of fruit on crust. Pour on cheese mixture.

5. Bake at 325 degrees F. for 40 minutes or until center is set. Remove from oven and cool.

6. Mix all glaze ingredients and simmer until thickened (about 5–10 minutes).

7. Arrange rest of fruit decoratively on top of cake. Pour on glaze evenly over fruit. Serve at room temperature. Serves 6–8.

Cook the fruit so that it is tender enough to cut with a fork, making it easier later to slice and eat. Any combination of fruit is feasible, but choosing those with contrasts in colors and tastes makes the cake more interesting. Dried fruit allows a "fruit" cake in the off season and becomes doubly appetizing in deepest January.

Fig and Ginger Cheese Tart

CRUST:

¾ C unbleached all-purpose
   flour
¼ C ground blanched almonds
½ t salt
⅓ C shortening
4 T cold water

FILLING:

1 C preserved figs, steamed,
   chopped
8 oz. cream cheese, softened
½ C sour cream
2 large eggs, slightly beaten
½ C sugar
¼ C candied ginger, finely
   chopped

GLAZE:

⅓ C apricot jam

1. For crust, mix flour, ground almonds, and salt. Cut in shortening. Stir in water one T at a time until dough forms a ball. Roll out and place in a 9-inch tart pan. Pierce with fork. Bake at 450 degrees F. for 7–9 minutes or until set. Cool.

2. For filling, steam figs over boiling water for 40 minutes or until softened and plumped. Chop into small pieces. Set aside.

3. Beat cheese and sour cream until smooth and light.

4. Beat in eggs. Mix in sugar and ginger. Pour into crust.

5. Place figs on cheese mixture (some will sink).

6. Bake at 350 degrees F. for 20 minutes or until cheese-mixture center is set. Remove from oven.

7. For glaze, heat apricot jam. Strain, if necessary. Brush over entire tart. Serves 6.

Since Imperial Roman times, figs have been prized for their tender sweetness, unlike the savor of any other fruit. They must ripen soft on the tree; a reason fresh figs are difficult to find far from their principal growing regions in the West and South. Dried figs may be plumped by boiling, but preserved figs, those that are packaged semidried, are best steamed.

Fruit-topped Cheesecake

CRUST:

1 C ground oats
¼ C brown sugar
½ t salt
½ t cinnamon
¼ C sweet butter, melted

FILLING:

1 lb. cream cheese, softened
14 oz. sweetened condensed
   milk
3 large eggs, separated
   rind and juice of 1 fresh
   lemon
¼ t salt

TOPPING:

2 C fresh fruit, peeled, pitted,
   diced
⅓ C sugar
1 T unbleached all-purpose
   flour
¼ t allspice
   water as needed

1. For crust, mix oats, sugar, salt, and cinnamon. Stir in butter. Press onto bottom and side of 9-inch springform pan. Bake at 450 degrees F. for 4 minutes or until set. Cool.

2. For filling, beat cheese until smooth and light. Blend in milk and egg yolks.

3. Stir in lemon rind and juice.

4. In separate bowl beat egg whites and salt until soft peaks form.

5. Fold whites into milk mixture. Pour into crust.

6. Bake at 300 degrees F. for 50 minutes or until center is set. Cool. Chill.

7. For topping, cook fruit, sugar, flour, allspice and small amount of water over medium heat until slightly tender. Remove pan side from cake. Spread fruit topping decoratively over cake. Serves 10–12.

Nearly any fruit is appropriate— peaches, pears, apples, cantaloupe. Let the syrup of the fruit drape over the side of the cake, which is light but firm. Cook the fruit only until tender, not so that it's mushy. Every fruit takes a different time, but none takes too long, so be on the alert.

Ginger Cheese Pie

CRUST:
- 1   C graham cracker crumbs
- ½   t cinnamon
- ¼   C sweet butter, melted

FILLING:
- 8   oz. cream cheese, softened
- ½   C sugar
- 2   large eggs, beaten
- 1   T freshly grated ginger

TOPPING:
- 1½   C sour cream
- 3   T sugar
- 1   T preserved ginger, finely
  chopped

1. For crust, mix crumbs with cinnamon. Stir in butter. Press into bottom and up side of 9-inch pie plate. Bake at 450 degrees F. for 4 minutes or until set. Cool.

2. For filling, beat cheese, sugar, and eggs.

3. Stir in grated ginger. Pour mixture into crust. Bake at 350 degrees F. for 20 minutes.

4. For topping, mix sour cream with sugar. Mix in preserved ginger.

5. Turn off oven and return pie to heat for 5 minutes. Cool. Chill. Serves 6.

The zing of ginger is well known but, unfortunately, ginger has lost its place in the kitchen. As in this recipe, it may be used effectively in sauces and roasts as well as in cookies and cakes.

Honey Almond Cheese Pie

CRUST:
- ¾ C unbleached all-purpose flour
- ¼ C graham flour
- ½ t salt
- ⅓ C shortening
- 4–5 T cold water

FILLING:
- 1 lb. ricotta
- ⅔ C honey
- 3 large eggs, slightly beaten
- ½ t freshly grated lemon peel
- ½ t freshly grated orange peel
- ¼ C blanched sliced almonds

1. For crust, mix flours and salt. Cut in shortening. Stir in water one T at a time until dough forms a ball. Roll out and place in a 9-inch pie plate. Pierce with fork. Bake at 450 degrees F. for 7–9 minutes or until lightly toasted. Cool.

2. For filling, beat ricotta until smooth and light. Beat in honey, eggs, lemon and orange peels until thoroughly mixed.

3. Pour into crust. Sprinkle on almond slices.

4. Bake at 350 degrees F. for 45 minutes or until center is set and the almonds and top are toasted. Cool. Serves 6.

This utterly simple pie makes a basic straightforward use of the oldest sweetening in history. The coarse-grained graham whole-wheat flour in the crust complements the almond slices.

Honey Cheesecake

CRUST:

¼ C ground walnuts
¼ C toasted wheat germ
½ C whole wheat flour
1 t honey
¼ C sweet butter, melted

FILLING:

1 lb. cream cheese, softened
⅔ C sour cream
¼ C unbleached all-purpose
   flour
¾ C honey
4 large eggs, separated
½ T almond extract
   grated rind of 1 lemon

1. For crust, mix walnuts, wheat germ, flour. Stir to dissolve honey in warm butter. Stir butter mixture into flour mixture. Press into bottom and up side of 8-inch springform pan. Bake at 450 degrees F. for 4 minutes or until set. Cool.

2. For filling, beat cheese, sour cream, flour, and honey until smooth and light.

3. Beat in egg yolks one at a time.

4. Blend in almond and lemon rind.

5. Beat whites until stiff but not dry. Fold into cheese mixture.

6. Pour into crust. Bake at 325 degrees F. for 60 minutes or until lightly browned and set. Cool in oven. Serves 8–10.

Since honey is made from the nectar of plants, the plants from which the beehive gets its nectar flavor the honey. The range of honey flavors reaches from clover to buckwheat, eucalyptus, raspberry, and white gum honey. Honey is broken down to an elementary food form by the bees. It is for this reason that we do not have to digest it ourselves; honey is absorbed directly through our stomach walls, and gives us immediate energy. In baking, honey produces a dark crust. It also adds a tastier sweetening, and keeps breads and cakes moist longer than most other sweeteners. For easier handling, always coat your measuring spoons and cups with oil before dipping them into honey.

Ice Cream "Cheesecake"

1   15-oz. can evaporated milk
¾   C sugar
⅛   t salt
8   oz. cream cheese, softened
     grated rind and juice of 1
         lemon
2   large eggs, slightly beaten
1   pint all-purpose cream

1. Place milk and sugar in saucepan over medium heat. Stir to dissolve. Add salt. Remove from heat and cool.

2. In large bowl beat cheese until smooth and light (add a little cream if necessary).

3. Add lemon rind and juice, eggs, and cream. Mix well.

4. Combine milk and cheese mixtures. Blend well.

5. Freeze in ice cream maker according to manufacturer's instructions. Makes about 2 quarts.

If you can't bear to carry on life without the lusciousness of a cheesecake taste, but can dispense with the cake, try this. You can also make it in refrigerator ice cube trays (without the cube dividers) by alternately half-freezing and whipping the mixture, although it won't be as smooth and light as when it's made in an ice cream freezer. Spreading softened ice cream in a baked pie crust and then freezing it slightly more makes a delicious ice cream cheese pie. A sprinkle of freshly grated lemon peel on top adds a nice summertime garnish and color.

Käsekuchen

CRUST:
- 1 C unbleached all-purpose flour
- 2 T sugar
- ¼ t salt
- ¼ C sweet butter, softened
- 1 egg, slightly beaten

CAKE:
- 1 lb. dry cottage cheese
- 1 C sweet butter
  grated rind of 1 lemon
- 1¾ C sugar, divided
- 7 eggs, separated
- 2 C blanched almonds, ground
- 1 16-oz. can pitted sour red cherries, drained

1. For crust, sift flour, sugar, and salt together. Cut in butter. Stir in egg and shape dough into ball. Chill. Roll dough to fit bottom only of a 9-inch springform pan. Pierce with fork. Bake at 450 degrees F. for 8–10 minutes or until lightly toasted. Cool. Butter sides of pan.
2. For cake, sieve cheese. Set aside.
3. Cream butter and lemon peel. Gradually add 1 C sugar.
4. Add egg yolks one at a time and beat in.
5. Stir in cheese and almonds thoroughly.
6. Beat egg whites until frothy. Gradually beat in ¾ C sugar until thickened.
7. Fold whites into cheese mixture.
8. Spread cherries evenly over crust. Carefully pour and spread cheese mixture evenly over cherries.
9. Bake at 300 degrees F. for 1 hour. Turn off heat and let cake stand in the closed oven 1 hour longer. Cool. Chill before removing pan. Serves 14–16.

This traditional German cheesecake is high and light and, when cut, reveals the colorful cherries and crisp bottom crust. Dusting the top decoratively with confectioners' sugar adds even more brightness to this festive cake.

Key Lime Cheese Pie

CRUST:
- 1   C unbleached all-purpose flour
- ½   t salt
- ⅓   C shortening
- 4   T cold water

FILLING:
- 8   oz. cream cheese, softened
- 2   large eggs
-     zest of 4 limes
-     juice and pulp of 4 limes (about ⅔ C)
- 14   oz. can of sweetened condensed milk
-     sweetened whipped cream
-     garnish (lime rind or almonds)

1. For crust, mix flour and salt. Cut in shortening. Stir in water one T at a time until dough forms a ball. Roll out and place in 9-inch pie plate. Pierce with fork. Bake at 450 degrees F. for 7–9 minutes or until lightly toasted. Cool.

2. For filling, cut cheese into small pieces and beat until smooth and light.

3. Add eggs one at a time and beat for 2 minutes.

4. Stir in zest, juice, and pulp of limes.

5. Pour in milk. Beat until well blended.

6. Pour into prepared crust. Refrigerate at least 3 hours (preferably overnight). When serving, top with sweetened whipped cream. Garnish with a sprinkle of lime rind or ground toasted almonds. Serves 6.

Any limes will do if you can't find those from around Key West, Florida, where the authentic Key lime pie originated. This variation produces an extremely creamy-textured pie with a zesty lime tartness balanced by the whipped cream. Great for the summer. Since limes contain about a third more citric acid than lemons, they were used by British sailors beginning in the mid-eighteenth century to ward off scurvy. Hence, an Englishman's nickname of limey. Condensed milk was first made in 1858, but exactly when condensed milk and limes were combined is buried in Florida tradition.

Lemon Cheesecake I

CRUST:

½ C Zwieback crumbs
1 C finely ground walnuts
3 T sugar
⅓ C sweet butter, melted

FILLING:

1½ lbs. cream cheese, softened
¾ C sugar
¼ t salt
1 t vanilla extract
    rind and juice of 1 large
    lemon
4 eggs, separated
1 C heavy cream, whipped
½ C unbleached all-purpose
    flour
    confectioners' sugar

1. For crust, mix Zwieback and walnut crumbs with sugar. Stir in butter. Press into bottom and up side of 9-inch springform pan. Bake at 450 degrees F. for 4 minutes or until set. Cool.

2. For filling, beat cheese, sugar, salt, vanilla, lemon rind and juice. Beat in egg yolks one at a time.

3. Whip whites until stiff but not dry.

4. Fold whites into cream. Fold flour into cream mixture. Fold cream mixture into cheese mixture.

5. Pour into crust. Bake at 325 degrees F. for 1 hour and 15 minutes. Turn off heat and keep in oven for 1 hour more with oven door closed. Then open oven door, and leave for 1 hour more. Remove cake from oven. Cool. Chill. Dust with confectioners' sugar. Serves 10–12.

Frequently, the lemon-flavored cheesecake is the basis of comparison with others. This one is typical: not too dense, but heavy enough to fulfill the image of cheesecake. The lemon taste is just overt enough to stand on its own.

Lemon Cheesecake II

CRUST:
- 1 C graham cracker crumbs
- 3 T sugar
- 1 t cinnamon
- ¼ C sweet butter, melted

FILLING:
- 1½ lbs. cottage cheese, sieved
- 3 large eggs
- ¾ C sugar
- ½ C unbleached all-purpose flour
- 1 t vanilla extract
  rind and juice of 1 large lemon
- 1½ C all-purpose cream

1. For crust, mix crumbs, sugar, and cinnamon. Stir in butter. Reserve 2 T. Press into bottom and up side of an 8-inch springform pan. Bake at 450 degrees F. for 4 minutes or until set. Cool.

2. For filling, beat cottage cheese, adding one egg at a time.

3. Blend in sugar, flour, vanilla, and lemon rind and juice. Beat well.

4. Stir in cream thoroughly.

5. Pour into crust. Sprinkle with reserved crumbs.

6. Bake at 325 degrees F. for 1 hour and 15 minutes or until center is set. Open oven door and allow cake to cool slowly for 1 hour more. Remove from oven and allow to cool to room temperature. Chill. Serves 10.

Lemons are believed to have been brought over by Columbus. Planted on Haiti, their pleasant usefulness spread throughout the Western Hemisphere. Now California grows the majority of lemons supplied for this country. There, lemons are harvested for nearly the entire year. The best way to compare lemons for juice content and freshness is to weigh them. This lemon-flavored cake is thick-textured but moderately light.

Lemon Cheese Pie

CRUST:

1¼	C unbleached all-purpose flour
¾	t salt
6	T shortening
4–5	T cold water

FILLING:

4	eggs
¾	C sugar
	dash of salt
	rind and juice of 1 large lemon
¾	C all-purpose cream
3	C cottage cheese, sieved
¼	C unbleached all-purpose flour

1. For crust, mix flour and salt. Cut in shortening. Stir in water one T at a time until dough forms a ball. Roll out and place in 9-inch pie plate. Pierce with fork. Bake at 450 degrees F. for 7–9 minutes or until lightly toasted. Cool.

2. For filling, beat eggs until foamy. Gradually add sugar and continue beating until thick and lemon-colored.

3. Blend in salt, the lemon juice only, and cream. Beat in cheese and flour.

4. Pour into crust. Bake at 350 degrees F. for 1 hour or until center is set.

5. Remove from oven and cool. Sprinkle top with grated lemon rind. Serves 6–8.

When grating a lemon, it's better to scrape only the yellow surface, taking as little of the white pulp as possible. The outer skin has what you want—the aromatic oils.

Lemonade Cheesecake

CRUST:

1¼ C chocolate wafer crumbs
⅓ C sweet butter, melted

FILLING:

¾ C milk
2 T unflavored gelatin
2 large eggs, separated
2 C ricotta
6 oz. frozen lemonade
   concentrate, thawed
¼ C sugar
1 C all-purpose cream,
   whipped

1. For crust, mix crumbs and butter. Reserve 2 T. Press into bottom and up side of 8-inch springform pan. Bake at 450 degrees F. for 4 minutes or until set. Cool.

2. For filling, place milk in saucepan and sprinkle on gelatin so that it partially dissolves. Stir in egg yolks.

3. Dissolve gelatin over medium heat, stirring constantly until mixture thickens. Remove from heat.

4. Blend ricotta and concentrate into gelatin mixture.

5. Beat egg whites until stiff. Gradually add sugar and beat until mixture thickens.

6. Fold whites into ricotta mixture. Fold in whipped cream.

7. Pour into crust. Sprinkle on reserved crumbs. Chill for at least 2 hours. Serves 6–8.

Gelatin is usually packaged in envelopes containing one tablespoon. It is up to 90 percent protein and is concentrated from an extract of beef bones and connective tissues. One tablespoon expands in moisture and heat, and then congeals about a pint of liquid when it cools.

Lime Pear Cheesecake

CRUST:
- 1 C unbleached all-purpose flour
  dash of salt
- 2 T sugar
- 1 C water
- ⅓ C sweet butter
- 4 large eggs

FILLING:
- 1½ T unflavored gelatin
- ¾ C sugar (plus 2 T)
- ¼ t salt
- 2 eggs, separated
- ¾ C milk
  grated rind and juice of 1 lime
- ¼ t almond extract
- 1 lb. ricotta
- ½ C all-purpose cream

TOPPING:
- 4 peeled pear halves
- 2 T sugar
  water to cover

GLAZE:
- ½ C pear syrup
- 1 T sugar
- 1 T (scant) cornstarch dissolved in 1 T water
  almond slices

1. For crust, mix flour, salt, and sugar. In large pan boil water and butter. Add flour, remove from burner, and immediately beat rapidly with wooden spoon until batter is smooth. Cool 2 minutes. Add eggs one at a time, beating in thoroughly. Spread this chou paste evenly on bottom and side of a well greased 9-inch springform pan. Bake at 400 degrees F. for 10 minutes, reducing heat to 350 for another 25 minutes or until firm and browned. Cool.

2. For filling, mix gelatin with sugar and salt.

3. Mix egg yolks with milk. Stir into gelatin mixture. Cook over medium heat, stirring, until mixture thickens. Remove from heat.

4. Add lime peel, lime juice, and almond extract. Stir in ricotta. Refrigerate for ½ hour to slightly solidify. Stir regularly.

5. Beat cream until soft peaks form.

6. Beat egg whites until soft peaks form. Add 2 T sugar and beat until thickened.

7. Fold cream and egg whites into ricotta mixture. Pour into crust. Chill 1 hour.

8. For topping, poach pear halves in sugared water for 5 minutes or until softened but still firm. Place pears decoratively on top of cake.

9. For glaze, mix pear syrup with sugar. Add cornstarch (mixed in 1 T water first) and boil until thickened and transparent. Brush on top of pears and cake top. Sprinkle on almond slices. Chill 2 hours or until firm. Remove pan side. Serves 8–10.

The bottom of the chou paste (the kind of dough used for cream puffs and eclairs) rises bubblelike. You may either cut some off or weight it down with a bowl before adding the filling. Lime, almonds, and pears (canned pears work too) form a well balanced combination, while the lightness of the ricotta filling makes this especially appealing for an unusual, elegant summer dessert.

Maple Ricotta Cheesecake

CRUST:

1	C vanilla wafer crumbs
3½	T sweet butter, melted

FILLING:

2	eggs, separated
⅓	C sugar
1	lb. dry ricotta
½	C unbleached all-purpose flour
½	C authentic maple syrup
¾	t vanilla extract
¼	t salt

1. For crust, mix crumbs and butter until thoroughly moist. Press into bottom and up side of 8-inch springform pan. Bake at 450 degrees F. for 4 minutes or until set. Cool.

2. For filling, beat egg whites until foamy. Add sugar and beat until thickened.

3. Place into blender ricotta, flour, egg yolks, maple syrup, vanilla, and salt. Whirl until smooth and light. Pour into bowl.

4. Fold whites into ricotta mixture. Pour into crust.

5. Bake at 350 degrees F. for 35 minutes or until golden and the center is set. Cool. Serves 6.

Maple syrup is one of the treasures of a kitchen cupboard. What is now called "pancake syrup," full of laboratory flavors, bears no resemblance whatsoever to syrup made entirely from the real sap from maple trees. Forty gallons of sap are boiled down to make one gallon of syrup, with the rich, complex, tasty flavors of maple sweetness. This cake is light, maple-y (but not too strong), and right on target for a New England–style dinner.

Neapolitan Cheesecake

CHOCOLATE:
6 oz. semisweet chocolate bits
1 T unflavored gelatin
2 T cold water
¼ C boiling water
¼ C dark brown sugar
½ t vanilla extract
1 large egg
8 oz. cream cheese, softened
⅓ C all-purpose cream

STRAWBERRY:
1½ C fresh strawberries, puréed
1 T unflavored gelatin
2 T cold water
¼ C boiling water
½ C sugar
8 oz. cream cheese, softened
⅓ C all-purpose cream
1 large egg

LEMON:
1 T unflavored gelatin
2 T cold water
2 t fresh lemon juice
¼ C boiling water
¼ C sugar
1 large egg
⅓ C all-purpose cream
8 oz. cream cheese, softened

1. For chocolate, melt chocolate bits over very low heat.
2. Soften gelatin in water. Pour into blender. Add boiling water, brown sugar, and vanilla, and whirl.
3. While blender is whirling, add egg, cheese piece by piece, and cream. Blend for 1 minute until smooth and light. Add melted chocolate and blend until well mixed. Pour into tight-fitting 8-inch springform pan. Chill until set (about 1–2 hours).
4. Later, for strawberry, mash and drain strawberries. Soften gelatin in water.
5. Pour gelatin into blender. Add boiling water and sugar. While whirling, add cheese piece by piece. Add cream and egg.
6. Pour in strawberries and whirl. Pour mixture gently over set chocolate layer. Chill until set (2–3 hours).
7. For lemon, dissolve gelatin in cold water. Pour into blender and add lemon juice, boiling water, and sugar. Whirl. With blender operating, add egg, cream, and cheese piece by piece. Whirl until smooth and light.
8. Pour very gently over soft strawberry layer. Chill until set (about 1–2 hours). Serve chilled. Serves 10–12.

Because strawberries resist gelatin, this colorful layered cake blossoms forth with the middle strawberry layer softer than the chocolate and lemon. Mousse-like, the strawberry layer adds a change in texture at the right place. Be sure to serve the cake chilled. You can tighten the strawberry layer with more gelatin, if you wish. This rendition takes relatively little actual working time because of the blender, although the overall time is extended waiting for the layers to set.

New York–Style Cheesecake I

CRUST:

1¼ C unbleached all-purpose flour
¼ C sugar
1 t grated lemon rind
½ C sweet butter, and butter for pan
1 egg yolk

FILLING:

2½ lbs. cream cheese, softened
1½ C sugar
¼ C unbleached all-purpose flour
   rind and juice of 1 large fresh lemon
½ t vanilla extract
5 whole large eggs
2 egg yolks
½ C heavy cream

1. For crust, mix flour, sugar, and lemon rind. Cut in butter. Blend in egg yolk. Add 1 T cream if necessary. Cover and chill.

2. Roll out chilled dough ⅛-inch thick. Place over buttered bottom of 9-inch springform pan. Trim off and reserve excess. Pierce with fork. Bake circle at 450 degrees F. for 7–9 minutes or until lightly toasted.

3. Butter side of pan and connect it to base. Roll out remaining dough ⅛-inch thick and cut it to fit the side. Press dough onto side and gently seal against bottom crust. (Trim later.)

4. For filling, blend cheese, sugar, flour, lemon rind and juice, and vanilla.

5. Beat in eggs and egg yolks one egg at a time.

6. Fold in cream. Pour into crust. Carefully trim excess side dough.

7. Bake at 500 degrees F. for 10 minutes. Reduce temperature to 250 degrees F. and continue baking for 1 hour more. Cool. Chill. Serves 10–12.

This is the large, heavier version of cheesecake found so prevalently in and around New York City. Lindy's restaurant was well known for this cheesecake. Most New York cakes have this rich thick crust. It's the kind of recipe that ends up with small narrow wedges that satisfy as if they were large ones. The rich concentration of cheese, cream, and eggs holds sway. To many people, this style has assumed the role of the classic cheesecake.

New York–Style Cheesecake II

CRUST:

1¼ C Zwieback crumbs
2   T sugar
⅓   C sweet butter, melted, and
    butter for pan

FILLING:

1   lb. cream cheese, softened
1   t vanilla extract
½   C sugar, divided
¼   C unbleached all-purpose
    flour
¼   t salt
4   egg yolks, slightly beaten
    rind and juice of 1 fresh
    lemon
1   C heavy cream
4   egg whites

1. For crust, mix crumbs and sugar. Stir in butter. Press into buttered 9-inch springform pan. Bake at 450 degrees F. for 4 minutes or until set. Cool.

2. For filling, beat cheese until smooth and light.

3. Blend in vanilla, ¼ C sugar, flour, and salt.

4. Beat in egg yolks. Stir in lemon rind and juice, and cream.

5. Beat egg whites until stiff. Gradually add ¼ C sugar and continue beating until thickened.

6. Fold meringue into cheese mixture. Pour into crust.

7. Bake at 325 degrees F. for 1½ hours or until set. Cool. Chill. Serves 10–12.

This is a rich cake, but by creating a meringue and folding it into the cheese mixture, a buoyancy is produced. The airiness makes the cake lighter than the usual New York Style.

New York–Style Cheesecake III

CRUST:
1	C unbleached all-purpose flour
3	T sugar
1	t fresh lemon rind
6	T sweet butter, and butter for pan
1	egg yolk
1–2	T heavy cream

FILLING:
1½	lbs. cream cheese, softened
1	C plus 2 T sugar
2	T unbleached all-purpose flour
	rind of 1 orange
	rind of 1 lemon
¼	t vanilla extract
4	large eggs
1	egg yolk
¼	C heavy cream

TOPPING:
2	ripe bananas
⅓	C apricot jam, strained

1. For crust, mix flour, sugar, and lemon rind. Cut in butter to make crumb mixture. Stir in egg yolk. Stir in cream to make dough form a ball. Chill 10–15 minutes. Roll out half of dough ⅛-inch thick and cover bottom of 8-inch springform pan. Pierce with fork. Bake at 450 degrees F. for 5–8 minutes or until very lightly browned. Cool.
2. Roll out remaining dough ⅛-inch thick. Butter inside rim of pan. Cut dough into strips. Place strips on rim, slightly overlapping and sealing to the bottom crust. (Trim later.)
3. For filling, cut cheese into small pieces. Beat into it sugar, flour, rinds, and vanilla.
4. Beat in whole eggs and yolk one at a time until well blended. Beat in cream.
5. Pour batter into crust. With sharp knife, cut away excess side crust above the filling.
6. Bake at 500 degrees F. for 10 minutes. Reduce heat to 200 degrees F. for 50 minutes or until center is set. Cool.
7. For topping, slice banana in ¼-inch thick circles and decoratively place overlapping in two circles inside the rim of the cake. Place 1 banana slice in center.
8. Heat jam and if necessary strain out large apricot sections. Brush jam on banana and outer rim of cake. Chill 2 hours. Serves 8–10.

A version of the classic New York cheesecake, this is rich, moist, and irresistible. If you beat the filling a little longer than needed to mix in the eggs, the cake turns out slightly more buoyant than most heavy New York styles. An easy way to fit the bottom crust is to place the dough over the pan (without the rim) and roll the pin hard over it. This cuts the dough perfectly to the bottom of the pan. The smaller size bananas make more fitting rounds (only 1½ bananas are needed). Use quality jam for the glaze to keep all parts of this cake in tandem with the rest of the best ingredients you can find.

Orange Cheese Pie

CRUST:
1½ C crushed coconut
      macaroons
  3 T sweet butter, melted (if
      needed)

FILLING:
  1 T unflavored gelatin
  ⅓ C sugar
  2 eggs, separated
  6 oz. frozen orange
      concentrate, thawed
  ⅓ C water
  1 lb. cottage cheese, sieved
  ¼ C sugar
  ½ C plain yogurt

1. For crust, grind crisp maca-roons with a blender. If the crumbs do not easily press into a 9-inch pie plate, moisten them with butter. Bake at 450 degrees F. for 4 minutes or until lightly toasted. Cool.

2. For filling, mix gelatin and ⅓ C sugar in a saucepan. Mix in egg yolks. Stir in orange juice and water. Bring to a simmer, stirring constantly. Remove from heat and cool so that it thickens slightly.

3. Transfer mixture to larger bowl. Add cottage cheese.

4. Beat egg whites until soft peaks form. Slowly add ¼ C sugar and continue beating until thickened. Fold into cheese mixture.

5. Fold yogurt into cheese mixture.

6. Pour into crust and refrigerate for 2 hours or until set. Serves 6.

Coconut and orange have always married well. Not only does this recipe make use of these two complementary tastes, but it also calls for their prepared forms. All you do is grind the macaroons for the underlying coconut flavor, and then thaw the orange juice concentrate for the theme taste. Sieving the cottage cheese through a food mill works well. Otherwise, you may scrape the cheese through a strainer for much the same effect. This dish owes more than a little to the edgy tang of the yogurt. It's a good, refreshing, nutritious pie.

Orange Sauce Cheesecake

CRUST:
1¼ C anisette toast crumbs
¼   C sweet butter, melted

FILLING:
1 lb. ricotta
2 large eggs
½ C honey
¼ C unbleached all-purpose
    flour
⅓ C sour cream
1 t vanilla extract
    dash of salt

SAUCE:
1 C water
⅓ C sugar
1 T cornstarch
⅓ C orange juice
    grated rind of 1 orange
1 t lemon juice

1. For crust, crush anisette toast to crumbs with rolling pin or food processor. In bowl pour butter over crumbs and mix well with fork. Chill. Press crumbs on bottom and up side of 8-inch springform pan. Bake at 450 degrees F. for 4 minutes or until set. Cool.

2. For filling, beat ricotta until smooth and light. Add eggs one at a time, beating well.

3. Beat in honey, flour, sour cream, vanilla, and salt.

4. Pour into crust. Bake at 325 degrees F. for 1 hour 20 minutes or until deep brown and done. Cool. Chill.

5. For sauce, boil ¾ C water and sugar until dissolved. Mix cornstarch in ¼ C water and add to sugar water. Simmer, stirring constantly. Add orange juice, rind, and lemon juice. Simmer, stirring constantly for about 5 minutes or until sauce is thick and transparent.

6. To serve, pour warm sauce over cake wedges. Serves 6.

Ricotta cheesecakes are light-tasting and easy on the palate. This thin one is no exception. The honey helps to toast the top a polished walnut color. When the sauce is poured over, the dish takes on an appetizing cheesecake variation that is not overly rich or intimidating to a weight-watcher. For the anisette toast, you might bake your own, or use the Stella Doro brand.

Paskha

1 C raisins
2 T sugar
¼ C water
1 C sour cream
1 lb. cream cheese, softened
1 C confectioners' sugar
½ t vanilla extract
½ t almond extract
   sliced blanched almonds
   sour cherries
2–4 T flour (if needed)

1. Soak raisins in sugar and water for half an hour.
2. Beat sour cream into cheese. Add confectioners' sugar, vanilla and almond extracts.
3. Drain raisins and mix into cheese mixture.
4. Form into pyramid. Chill overnight. Garnish with almonds on side, cherries on top. Serves 4–6.

This unbaked Russian cake (*paskha* means Easter in Russian) is traditionally formed into a straight-sided pyramid. The mixture should be firm. If it appears that it won't be while you're preparing it, then add a small amount of flour (two to four tablespoons) to the cheese mixture.

Peach Cheese Pie

CRUST:

¾   C unbleached all-purpose
     flour
¼   C ground blanched almonds
½   t salt
2   T sweet butter
3   T shortening
4   T cold water

FILLING:

8   oz. cream cheese, softened
2   large eggs
½   C sugar
1   t vanilla extract
1   T minced candied ginger
3   Clingstone peaches, peeled,
     pitted, sliced (reserve
     juice)

GLAZE:

1   T cornstarch
¼   C sugar
1   C reserved peach juice
1   t fresh lemon juice
⅛   t almond extract
     whipped cream

1. For crust, mix flour, almonds, and salt. Cut in butter and shortening. Stir in water one T at a time until dough forms a ball. Roll out and place in 9-inch pie plate.

Pierce with fork. Bake at 450 degrees F. for 7–9 minutes or until lightly toasted. Cool.

2. For filling, beat cheese until smooth and light. Beat in eggs one at a time until thoroughly blended. Beat in sugar, vanilla, and ginger.

3. Pour into crust. Bake at 375 degrees F. for 30 minutes or until center is set. Cool.

4. Cover peach slices in large skillet with water and poach until slightly soft. Don't overcook. Drain and reserve juice.

5. Arrange peach slices decoratively on cooled pie.

6. For glaze, mix cornstarch and sugar in small saucepan. Stir in 1 C peach juice, lemon juice, and almond extract. Stirring constantly, cook over medium heat until thickened.

7. Pour glaze over peaches. Chill. Garnish with dollops of sweetened whipped cream before serving. Serves 6–8.

A tree-ripened peach (before the machines remove the natural fuzz!) is one of the succulent delights of the tongue. Picked green, a peach doesn't ripen further; it merely dries up. Originally from China, the peach represents both immortality and springtime. In European Christian paintings and stained glass, a peach is a sign of salvation. Good fresh peaches, like Elberta, Clingstone, and Freestone, are especially complemented with almond tastes, which this recipe calls for.

Peach Cheese Tart

CRUST:

1 C unbleached all-purpose
    flour
½ t salt
⅓ C shortening
4 T cold water
    egg white

FILLING:

2 T cornstarch
1¼ C sugar, divided
1 C ricotta
1 C hot milk
3 egg yolks, slightly beaten
1 T sweet sherry
2 C water
1 t fresh lemon juice
2 C peaches, sliced, peeled,
    pitted

1. For crust, mix flour and salt. Cut in shortening. Stir in water one T at a time until dough forms a ball. Roll out and place in a 9-inch tart pan. Pierce with fork.

Brush bottom with egg white. Bake at 450 degrees F. for 7–9 minutes or until moderately toasted. Cool.

2. For filling, mix cornstarch and ½ C sugar. Blend in ricotta.

3. Gradually stir in milk and cook over low heat until thickened, stirring constantly.

4. Place in double-boiler and cook another 10 minutes.

5. Add some cheese mixture to egg yolks and stir constantly. Pour yolks into mixture and cook over hot water 2 minutes, stirring constantly.

6. Remove mixture from heat. Stir in sherry.

7. Pour into crust.

8. Mix remaining sugar, water, and lemon juice in saucepan. Cook covered on stove top 5 minutes.

9. Stir in peaches and cook 10 minutes.

10. Remove peaches and cool. Continue cooking syrup-glaze until it thickens.

11. Place peaches decoratively on cheese mixture.

12. Gently brush glaze over peaches. Cool. Serves 6.

This method is similar to the classic pastry—cream tarts. The cream is prepared separately from the poached fruit. It's then placed in the baked crust, the fruit is placed on it, and the glaze is brushed on as the final step. Other fruits may be easily substituted for this ever-delicious tart.

Peanut Butter and Red Raspberry Jelly Cheesecake

CRUST:
1 C vanilla wafer crumbs
2 T light brown sugar
3 T sweet butter, melted

FILLING:
1 lb. cream cheese, softened
1 C sugar
½ C all-natural crunchy peanut butter
3 T unbleached all-purpose flour
4 large eggs, slightly beaten
½ C light cream

GLAZE:
½ C red raspberry jelly

1. For crust, mix crumbs, brown sugar, and melted butter. Press mixture on bottom and up side of 9-inch springform pan. Bake at 450 degrees F. for 4 minutes or until set. Cool.

2. For filling, beat cream cheese until smooth and light. Mix in sugar, peanut butter, and flour until well blended.

3. Add eggs and blend well.

4. Stir in cream.

5. Pour mixture into crust. Bake at 325 degrees F. for 45–55 minutes or until center is set. Cool. Remove rim from pan.

6. For glaze, heat jelly until melted. Pour and smooth over cake. Chill. Serves 8–10.

Homemade peanut butter is nothing more than two tablespoons of vegetable oil to every cup of salted peanuts, whirled in a blender. Making your own guarantees fresh wholesome peanut butter. Commercial peanut butter, on the other hand, may have 10 percent of its bulk devoted to hydrogenated shortening, corn syrup, sugar, antioxidants, and other additions, all of which reduce taste and nutrition. This dish is a far better creation than it may first appear, especially if you make your own red raspberry jelly, too.

Pineapple Apricot Cheesecake

1½ C canned pitted apricot
    halves, drained (reserve
    juice)
¾ t salt
2 C ricotta
4 slices canned pineapple,
    drained (reserve juice)
¼ C pineapple juice
¼ C apricot juice
1 T unflavored gelatin
    juice and rind of 1 lime
½ C sugar
1 C heavy cream, whipped
    butter for pan

1. Press apricots through a food mill or sieve. Stir in salt and ricotta.
2. Heat combined pineapple and apricot juices to boil. Dissolve gelatin in them. Add lime juice and rind and sugar. Cool slightly.
3. Combine ricotta and gelatin mixtures. Fold in whipped cream.
4. Pour batter into buttered 8-inch springform pan. (Place pan on plate if not tight fitting.) Chill for 2 hours.
5. Place pineapple slices on top of cake. Chill another hour.
6. Remove side of pan before serving. Serves 6–8.

No-bake and no-crust, this light cake is a good one for a hot summer day. You may substitute lemon for the lime, but the latter gives the cake a half-hidden undertaste that adds a softer complement to the apricot and pineapple juices.

Pineapple Banana Cheese Pie

CRUST:
- 1 C finely ground rolled oats
- 3 T brown sugar
- ¼ C sweet butter, melted

FILLING:
- 1 C drained crushed pineapple (reserve juice)
- ⅓ C sugar
- ¼ t salt
- 1 large egg, slightly beaten
- 1 T unflavored gelatin
- ¼ C cold water
- 1 C cottage cheese
- ⅔ C sour cream
- 1 t vanilla extract
- 1 ripe banana

GLAZE:
- reserved pineapple juice
- 1 T corn syrup
- 1 T sugar
- ½ T cornstarch dissolved in 2 T water

1. For crust, mix oats (which may be ground in a blender or food processor) with sugar. Stir in butter. Press in 9-inch pie plate. Bake at 450 degrees F. for 4 minutes or until moderately toasted.

2. For filling, combine pineapple, sugar, salt, and egg in saucepan. Heat over medium heat, stirring constantly. Dissolve gelatin in water and add. Cook until thickened. Remove from heat.

3. Combine cottage cheese, sour cream, and vanilla. Beat for 1–2 minutes.

4. Combine cheese and pineapple mixtures. Pour into prepared crust. Refrigerate until set, about 1–2 hours.

5. Slice banana in thin rounds and place them decoratively on pie.

6. For glaze, place reserved juice, corn syrup, sugar, and cornstarch in small saucepan. Stirring constantly, heat until transparent and slightly thickened. Brush or pour glaze over bananas. Chill. Serves 6.

We think of Hawaii as the place of origin of pineapple, but not so. Pineapple was imported to Hawaii, but from where no one knows for certain. Spanish explorers named the tropical fruit after its resemblance to a pine cone. Pineapple is one of the rare cases in which the canned version is selected from more choice fruits than the fresh product shipped to market. Pineapple loses its natural sweetness very quickly once picked, and therefore must be picked green for market. It never ripens to full potential, although the fruit may appear to be perfect. Fresh pineapple at a market has less than 4 percent natural sugar; pineapple canned the day it is picked has more than 12 percent.

Pineapple Cheesecake

CAKE:

¼ lb. sweet butter, softened, and butter for pan
1⅓ C light brown sugar
2¼ C cake flour, and flour for pan
1 t baking soda
½ t salt
1 t cinnamon
2 large eggs, slightly beaten
½ C milk
1 C ricotta
¼ C crushed pineapple, drained

GLAZE:

¼ C sweet butter
⅔ C light brown sugar
½ C crushed pineapple, drained
⅓ C flaked coconut
1 T pineapple juice
¼ t allspice

1. For cake, cream butter and sugar. Mix flour with soda, salt, and cinnamon and set aside.
2. Beat eggs into butter mixture one at a time.
3. Add flour alternately with milk, beginning and ending with flour.
4. Stir in ricotta and pineapple.
5. Pour mixture into well buttered, lightly floured 9-inch-square pan, 2 inches deep. Bake at 350 degrees F. for 40 minutes or until center is set.
6. Remove cake from oven and cool.
7. For glaze, cream butter and sugar. Blend in pineapple, coconut, juice, and allspice. Spread over cake. Broil 2–3 minutes or until golden. Serves 6.

Long used as table decorations, the pineapple evolved into a symbol of hospitality. Its image is seen on door lintels, wrought iron gates, church steeples and windows, for the pineapple is a sign of friendliness and welcome throughout the South and New England. Brown sugar and pineapple go well together, as in this simple coffee-cake-type recipe.

Pineapple Pecan Cheese Tart

CRUST:

1	C unbleached all-purpose flour
½	t salt
⅓	C shortening
3–4	T brandy

FILLING:

¼	lb. Gourmandaise cherry-flavored cheese, softened
½	C ricotta
½	C brown sugar
2	large eggs
4	pineapple slices
	pecans
2	T ground pecans
1	T brown sugar
½	t coriander

1. For crust, mix flour and salt. Cut in shortening. Stir in brandy one T at a time until dough forms a ball. Roll out and place in a 9-inch tart pan.

2. For filling, beat Gourmandaise and ricotta until smooth and light.

3. Beat in sugar and eggs for 3 minutes. Pour into crust.

4. Gently place pineapple slices on cheese mixture. Place pecan halves decoratively in the pineapple center holes and around edges.

5. Mix ground pecans, sugar, and coriander. Sprinkle over entire top of tart.

6. Bake at 450 degrees F. for 10 minutes. Reduce temperature to 350 degrees F. and continue baking for 20 minutes or until richly toasted. Serves 6.

Gourmandaise is a French dessert cheese flavored with cherry-tasting Kirsch liqueur. Specify cherry-, not walnut-flavored Gourmandaise, since cherries complement pineapple better than walnuts do, and won't detract from the more subtle pecan taste.

Plum Cheese Pie

CRUST:
1   C finely ground rolled oats
¼   C brown sugar
¼   C sweet butter, melted

FILLING:
2   C Italian plums (about 12)
     peeled, pitted, chopped
¾   C sugar, divided
2   T unbleached all-purpose
     flour
8   oz. cream cheese, softened
1   T lemon juice
¼   t salt
¼   C sour cream
2   eggs, separated

1. For crust, mix ground oats with sugar. Stir in butter. Press into bottom and side of 9-inch pie plate. Bake at 450 degrees F. for 4 minutes or until lightly toasted. Cool.

2. For filling, place plums, ½ C sugar, and flour in saucepan over medium-high heat. Stirring occasionally, cook until plums are slightly tender and sugar is dissolved. Remove from heat.

3. Beat cream cheese, lemon juice, salt, and sour cream until smooth and light. Add ¼ C sugar and egg yolks, and beat well.

4. Beat egg whites until stiff. Fold into cheese mixture.

5. Spread plum mixture on crust. Spread cheese mixture on top of plums.

6. Bake at 350 degrees F. for 20 minutes. Turn off heat and keep in oven for 10–15 minutes more or until pie is richly toasted but not cracked on top. Cool. Serve at room temperature. Serves 6.

To facilitate peeling the plums (the "before" version of prunes) soak them in very hot water for a few minutes. This loosens the skin somewhat. Graham cracker crumbs are a good substitute if you don't have means of finely grinding rolled oats. This dish is a pleasant combination of a light airy cheese top over a surprisingly mellow fresh plum taste.

Praline Cheesecake

CRUST:
1   C butter cookie crumbs
¼   C sweet butter, melted

FILLING:
1   C semisweet chocolate chips,
     melted
8   oz. cream cheese, softened
2   large eggs, separated
½   C dark brown sugar
⅛   t salt
½   C sour cream
2   T unbleached all-purpose
     flour
2   T dark brown sugar
1   t vanilla extract
1   T confectioners' sugar

1. For crust, stir crumbs and butter together. Press crumbs onto bottom and up side of 8-inch springform pan. Bake at 450 degrees F. for 4 minutes or until set. Cool.

2. For filling, melt chocolate bits in double boiler. Cool.

3. Cut up cream cheese into large mixing bowl. Add egg yolks, ½ C sugar, salt, sour cream and blend until smooth.

4. Stir in flour.

5. Beat egg whites until soft peaks form. Add 2 T sugar and beat until thickened. Add vanilla.

6. Stir chocolate into cheese mixture.

7. Fold in egg white mixture.

8. Pour into crust. Bake at 300 degrees F. for 40–50 minutes or until center is set. Cool.

9. Sprinkle with confectioners' sugar. Serves 10.

This comes out as a relatively thin cake. It is rich, moist, and nutmeg-dark, with a sumptuous, somewhat fudgy taste. A little of this goes a long way after a light meal. Look for butter cookies made with real butter, such as the Petite Beurre from Canada. This cake may be eaten warm, too.

Prune Cheese Pie

CRUST:

1½ C unbleached all-purpose
    flour
 ¾ C light brown sugar, firmly
    packed
 ½ t salt
 ¾ C sweet butter
1½ C shredded Cheddar cheese

FILLING:

 2 C chopped cooked pitted
    prunes
 ½ C chopped walnuts
 ½ t coriander
    sweetened whipped cream

1. For crust, combine flour, sugar, and salt. Cut in butter and cheese until fine particles are formed. Press ⅔ of the mixture into a 9-inch pie plate. Bake at 450 degrees F. for 5 minutes or until set. Cool.
2. For filling, fill crust with prunes and walnuts.
3. Mix coriander into remaining crumbs and spread over prunes.
4. Bake at 350 degrees F. for 25 minutes or until crumbs are toasted.
5. Cool slightly. Cut into slender wedges and serve warm with dollops of whipped cream. Serves 8–10.

Prunes are dried plums. After reaching full ripeness, they are dipped in lye, their skins are broken, and they are dried in the sun or in a kiln. Rehydrated, prunes contain much concentrated fructose, and have a taste that makes them versatile, both in their dark color and their mellow texture.

Pumpkin Chiffon Cheesecake

CRUST:

1 C vanilla wafer crumbs
2 T sugar
1 t allspice
¼ C sweet butter, melted

FILLING:

3 eggs, separated
2 C pumpkin, cooked and puréed
½ C unbleached all-purpose flour
10 oz. dry ricotta
3 oz. cream cheese, softened
½ C sugar
⅛ t salt
1 T blackstrap molasses
2 T brandy

1. For crust, mix crumbs, sugar, allspice, and melted butter. Press onto bottom and up side of 8-inch springform pan. Bake at 450 degrees F. for 4 minutes or until set. Cool.

2. For filling, beat egg whites until stiff.

3. Into blender place pumpkin, flour, egg yolks, ricotta, cream cheese, sugar, salt, molasses, and brandy. Whirl until smooth and light (about 1 minute).

4. Fold whites into mixture. Pour into crust.

5. Bake at 325 degrees F. for 30–40 minutes or until center is set. Serves 10.

Pumpkin is a most versatile vegetable of the gourd family. It's delicious as a soup, baked in cubes with bacon and mild cheese, mashed, stewed, or served many other ways, including as a cheesecake. This light, airy rendition calls for already prepared pumpkin, but fixing your own from fresh pumpkin is easy. Although pumpkins are grown up to a hundred pounds, the moderate basketball-size specimens are said by New England folks to be the tastiest.

Pumpkin Rum Cheese Pie

CRUST:

1 C unbleached all-purpose flour
½ t salt
½ t allspice
⅓ C shortening
2–4 T cold water

FILLING:

8 oz. cream cheese, softened
¾ C sugar, divided
2 large eggs
¾ t vanilla extract
1¼ C fresh pumpkin, cooked and puréed
2 T blackstrap molasses
2 T dark rum
1 t cinnamon
¼ t freshly grated nutmeg
¼ t cloves
  dash of salt
1 C evaporated milk

1. For crust, mix flour, salt, and allspice. Cut in shortening. Stir in water one T at a time to form dough into ball. Roll out and place in 9-inch pie plate. Pierce with fork. Bake at 450 degrees F. for 7–9 minutes or until lightly toasted. Cool.

2. For filling, cut up cheese into bowl. Add ¼ C sugar, 1 egg, and vanilla. Beat with electric mixer until smooth and light.

3. Spread cheese mixture on bottom of pie shell. Set aside.

4. Into blender, place all remaining ingredients—pumpkin, 1 egg, molasses, rum, cinnamon, nutmeg, cloves, salt, milk, and ½ C sugar. Whirl until well blended.

5. Pour carefully over cheese mixture.

6. Bake at 350 degrees F. for 50–60 minutes or until center is set. Cool. Serves 5–6.

This pie is a good way to recycle your Halloween pumpkin. A quick method to soften cream cheese from the refrigerator is to submerge it, foil and all, into a bowl of warm water. As for the pumpkin, peel, cube, and boil it until soft. Or cut it in half, scoop out the seeds, place cut-side down on a baking sheet, and bake it at 350 degrees F. until the pulp is soft. Then purée the pumpkin. Do this once and the freshness will persuade you never to throw your Halloween pumpkin out again.

Red Raspberry and Black Currant Tart

CRUST:
1¼ C butter cookie crumbs
¼   C sweet butter, melted

FILLING:
1   C red raspberries
⅔   C sugar, divided
½   C black currants
⅓   lb. Brie cheese, crust
     removed, softened
½   C ricotta
2   large eggs, slightly beaten

GLAZE:
⅓   C red currant jelly

1. For crust, mix crumbs and butter together. Press into 9-inch tart pan. Bake at 450 degrees F. for 4 minutes or until set. Cool.

2. For filling, sprinkle raspberries with ¼ C sugar. Set aside with black currants.

3. Blend Brie and ricotta cheeses.

4. Beat in eggs and rest of sugar. Pour into crust.

5. Gently place on raspberries. Decoratively sprinkle on currants.

6. Bake at 350 degrees F. for 30 minutes or until center is set.

7. For glaze, heat red currant jelly. Gently brush on tart. Cool. Serves 6.

The crust on Brie is edible, but it is not for this tart. Brie is a cow's milk cheese from France. When good and fresh, it should have a mild, creamy, slightly piquant undertaste. If you use frozen raspberries for this recipe, omit the sugaring of the fruit, since the frozen ones are already sweetened.

Red Raspberry Cheesecake

CAKE:

3 C ricotta
5 large eggs, slightly beaten
¼ t salt
1 t vanilla extract
¼ t almond extract
1 C sugar
¾ C unbleached all-purpose
   flour
1½ C milk

GLAZE:

½ C seedless raspberry jam
½ t lemon juice
¼ t vanilla extract

1. For cake, combine ricotta, eggs, salt, vanilla and almond extracts. Beat until well blended.

2. Mix sugar and flour. Lightly blend into cheese mixture. Stir in milk.

3. Pour into buttered 9-inch-square baking pan, 2 inches deep. Set dish in pan of water.

4. Bake at 350 degrees F. for 1 hour or until center is set. Cool.

5. For glaze, combine jam, lemon juice, and vanilla. Stir and heat to lukewarm. Pour on individual servings. Serves 9.

Delicate red raspberries are difficult to surpass for their light meadow-conjuring flavor. Raspberries may also be amber, purple, and black. Their near relations include dewberries, loganberries, boysenberries, and wineberries. Red raspberries, however, carry a special fragility when they're fresh, and hold onto their subtle flavor even when made into jams and jellies.

Red Raspberry Ricotta Cake

2 large eggs, separated
1 C sugar, divided
1 lb. ricotta
2 t vanilla extract
¼ t salt
½ C unbleached all-purpose
   flour
½ C all-purpose cream
2 T fresh lemon juice
   butter for pan
   raspberries (10 oz. frozen
   package), thawed

1. Beat egg whites until frothy. Add ⅓ C sugar and beat until thick.
2. Combine cheese with egg yolks, vanilla, salt, flour, ⅔ C sugar, cream, and lemon juice.
3. Fold in whites. Pour into 8-inch buttered springform pan.
4. Bake at 325 degrees F. for 1 hour or until center is set. Cool.
5. Cook raspberries until thickened slightly (about 10 minutes).
6. Spread raspberries over top of cake. Chill. Serves 6.

If you're looking for a light-tasting, crustless cheesecake that's easy to prepare and attractive as well, this is one. The delicacy of ricotta is nicely offset by the splendor of the raspberry topping. Use a tight-fitting springform pan, or place the pan on a baking sheet, to avoid the ricotta whey dripping through onto thé oven. The cake falls like a soufflé as it cools, to produce a modest-sized dessert best suited for a lunch or late afternoon snack.

Very Good!

Rhubarb Cheese Pie

CRUST:

 1   C unbleached all-purpose
     flour
 ½   t salt
 ⅓   C shortening
 4   T cold water

FILLING:

 2   C rhubarb, cut into 1-inch
     sections
 1   C sugar, divided
 1½ T cornstarch
     dash of salt
 8   oz. cream cheese, softened
 2   large eggs, slightly beaten
 ½   C sour cream
     slivered almonds

1. For crust, mix flour and salt. Cut in shortening. Stir in water one T at a time until dough forms a ball. Roll out and place in 9-inch pie plate. Pierce with fork. Bake at 450 degrees F. for 7–9 minutes or until lightly toasted. Cool.

2. For filling, mix rhubarb, ½ C sugar, cornstarch, and salt in a saucepan. Stirring regularly, cook until mixture boils and thickens. Pour into crust. Bake at 350 degrees F. for 10 minutes. Remove from oven.

3. Beat cheese, eggs, and ½ C sugar until smooth and light. Pour gently over rhubarb mixture.

4. Bake at 350 degrees F. for 30–35 minutes more. Cool. Chill.

5. Spread sour cream on top of pie. Sprinkle on almonds. Serves 6–8.

The best rhubarb is the young, relatively thin, reddish stalks. The old, longer stalks are stringier and often need peeling. The rhubarb plant leaves contain oxalic acid, a poison, and should never be eaten or used in cooking. Rhubarb has a high percentage of moisture and therefore doesn't need water in cooking. One cup of strawberries may replace a cup of rhubarb in this recipe for a nice complementary relationship of tastes.

Rhubarb Strawberry Tart

CRUST:

1 C unbleached all-purpose
  flour
½ t salt
⅓ C shortening
4–5 T cold water

FILLING:

1 C fresh rhubarb, cut into
  ½-inch sections
¾ C sugar, divided
¼ C water
1 C strawberries, sliced in
  half, sugared
1 C ricotta
2 large eggs, slightly beaten
½ C light cream
1 t mace
  grated rind of 1 orange

1. For crust, mix flour and salt. Cut in shortening. Stir in water one T at a time until dough forms a ball. Roll out and place in 9-inch high-sided tart pan. Pierce with fork. Bake at 450 degrees F. for 7–9 minutes or until lightly toasted. Cool.

2. For filling, mix rhubarb and ½ C sugar in saucepan and cook over medium heat until tender. Set aside with strawberries.

3. Beat ricotta and eggs. Stir in ¼ C sugar, cream, mace, and orange rind.

4. Pour cheese mixture into crust.

5. Combine rhubarb and strawberries. Place carefully on cheese mixture.

6. Bake at 350 degrees F. for 25 minutes or until cheese mixture in center is set. Serves 6.

The rhubarb-strawberry combination is a time-honored pairing, and difficult to top, especially with fresh fruit in early summer. The addition of grated rind of a large orange adds a further dimension to the undertaste. Served with scoops of fresh, rich, homemade vanilla ice cream, this one ushers in midsummer.

Rice Cheesecake

CAKE:
- 3   **large eggs, slightly beaten**
- 1   **C sugar**
- 1½ **C ricotta**
- ½   **C milk**
-      **grated rind of 1 large lemon**
- 4   **C cooked rice**
-      **butter for pan**

SAUCE:
- ⅓   **C sugar**
- 1   **T cornstarch**
- 1   **C water**
- 2   **T sweet butter**
-      **grated rind of 1 lime**
-      **juice of 1 fresh lime**
-      **dash of salt**

1. For cake, beat eggs and sugar together until well blended.

2. Combine ricotta with milk and lemon peel. Stir into egg mixture and beat until smooth.

3. Mix in rice.

4. Pour into buttered 9-inch-square baking pan.

5. Bake at 350 degrees F. for 45 minutes or until center is set.

6. For sauce, thicken sugar, cornstarch, and water in saucepan over boiling water. Remove from heat and blend in butter, rind, and juice of lime, and salt.

7. Serve cake warm, draped with lime sauce. Serves 9.

Sixty percent of the total human population eats rice. It is an immensely important food. The Chinese greet each other with, "Have you eaten your rice?" while the Japanese say that rice is the most sacred of all things after the Emperor. Whether they know it or not, Americans throw rice at weddings as an old symbol of fertility. The United States exports a huge quantity of rice, most of it grown in the South. We usually eat rice either boiled and topped with butter or as a pudding. This dish helps to enlarge our rice repertoire.

Rice Ricotta Cake

1   C rice, cooked in salted
        water
¼   lb. sweet butter, melted, and
        butter for pan
4   large eggs, slightly beaten
1½   C sugar
½   C ricotta
½   C white vermouth
        grated rind of 1 lemon

1. Cook rice according to directions. Cool.

2. Stir in butter.

3. Mix in eggs, sugar, ricotta, vermouth, and lemon peel.

4. Pour into buttered 8-inch springform pan. Bake at 350 degrees F. for 60 minutes or until golden. Serves 10.

This Italian *torta al riso* is a holiday dish that is easy and quick to prepare, proving that good ingredients make good cakes, whether they're fancy or not. This may be baked in a 9-inch square pan, and will be flatter than it would be if the pan were smaller. A light sprinkling of confectioners' sugar, plus a cherry or cranberry in the center, adds a flourish.

Ricotta Cheese Pie

CRUST:
- 1   C unbleached all-purpose flour
- ½   t salt
- ⅓   C shortening
- 3-4   T sweet sherry

FILLING:
- 1   lb. ricotta
- ¼   C sugar
- ⅓   C semisweet chocolate, chopped
- ¾   t almond extract grated rind of 1 orange
- 3   large eggs, slightly beaten
- ⅓   C blanched ground almonds

1. For crust, mix flour and salt. Cut in shortening. Stir in sherry one T at a time until dough forms a ball. Roll out and place in 9-inch tart pan. Pierce with fork. Bake at 450 degrees F. for 7–9 minutes or until lightly toasted. Cool.

2. For filling, beat ricotta until smooth and light.

3. Beat in sugar, chocolate, almond extract, orange peel, and eggs.

4. Pour into crust. Sprinkle almonds over top.

5. Bake at 350 degrees F. for 45 minutes or until center is set. Chill. Serves 6.

This Italian-style cheese pie has a crunchy almond top over a moderately rich center. The kaleidoscopic tastes of this dish fit it best for a casual dinner or buffet. It's also perfect for a light holiday celebration where the other dishes are just as multifaceted.

Sour Cream Cheesecake

CRUST:
1¼   C Zwieback crumbs
2   T sugar
3½   T sweet butter, melted

FILLING:
1   lb. cream cheese, softened
½   C sugar
¼   t allspice
½   t vanilla extract
     grated rind and juice of 1
        lemon
2   large eggs, separated

TOPPING:
1   C sour cream
1   T sugar
1   t vanilla extract

1. For crust, mix crumbs and sugar. Stir in butter. Press into bottom of 8-inch springform pan. Bake at 450 degrees F. for 4 minutes or until set. Cool.

2. For filling, blend cheese with sugar, allspice, vanilla, lemon rind and juice.

3. Add egg yolks individually, mixing well after each.

4. Beat egg whites until stiff. Fold into cheese mixture. Pour into crust.

5. Bake at 325 degrees F. for 45 minutes or until center is set.

6. For topping, blend sour cream with sugar and vanilla. Carefully spread over cake.

7. Return to oven for 8–10 minutes or until set. Cool before removing side of pan. Serves 6–8.

This is a light, moist version of the familiar classic lemon cheesecake. Placing the sour cream on top rather than inside the cake distinguishes the tastes more clearly. Allspice, used here, has cinnamon and clove hints. The allspice berry comes from the pimento tree, but is unrelated to the sweet Spanish pimento, which is a pepper.

Squash Maple Cheesecake

CRUST:
1 C finely crushed gingersnap
   crumbs
3½ T sweet butter, melted

FILLING:
¼ C authentic maple syrup
1 lb. cream cheese, softened
3 large eggs
¾ C sugar
2 C fresh squash purée
¾ t cinnamon
½ t allspice
¼ t coriander
¼ C heavy cream

TOPPING:
1¼ C sour cream
2 T sugar
1 t vanilla extract

1. For crust, mix crumbs with butter. Press onto bottom and up side of 8-inch springform pan. Bake at 450 degrees F. for 4 minutes or until set. Cool.

2. For filling, blend maple syrup into cream cheese.

3. Beat in eggs one at a time.

4. Add sugar.

5. Stir in squash, cinnamon, allspice, and coriander. Beat well.

6. Whip heavy cream slightly. Fold into cheese mixture. Pour into crust.

7. Bake at 325 degrees F. for 1 hour and 10 minutes or until center is set. Top toasts lightly and cracks slightly.

8. For topping, mix sour cream, sugar, and vanilla. Spread on top of cake. Bake 8–10 minutes more or until set. Don't overbake.

9. Turn off oven heat and open the door. Keep cake in the oven for half an hour or more. Remove and cool. May be served at room temperature or chilled. Serves 10.

The best time to make this creamy, moist cake is in the fall at harvest festival time—as an unusual but appropriate addition to a Thanksgiving meal. The spicy gingersnap crust, set against the autumn color of the squash cake, is perfect. You can make fresh squash purée easily. Simply peel a buttercup or similar yellow squash, cut it into chunks, and boil it until tender. Drain and run the chunks through a food mill to purée. Or cut a squash in half, scoop out seeds, place on baking sheet cut side down, and bake at 350 degrees F. until pulp is soft. Then purée the pulp.

Strawberry Cheesecake

CRUST:

1 C Zwieback crumbs
3 T sugar
3½ T sweet butter, melted

FILLING:

1 T unflavored gelatin
6 oz. cranberry juice
⅓ C sugar
½ t salt
  grated rind and juice of 1
    lemon
2 C cottage cheese
1 C all-purpose cream
3 C strawberries

1. For crust, blend crumbs and sugar. Stir in butter. Press into bottom and up side of buttered 8-inch springform pan. Bake at 450 degrees F. for 4 minutes or until set. Cool.
2. For filling, soften gelatin in juice for 5 minutes. Dissolve gelatin over low heat, stirring constantly.
3. Mix in sugar, salt, lemon rind and juice. Cool to room temperature.
4. Half at a time, whirl cottage cheese and gelatin mixture in blender.
5. Whip cream and fold into gelatin-cheese mixture. Chill until set.
6. Prepare strawberries by washing, removing hulls, and slicing. Fold into cheese mixture. Pour into crust. Chill. Serves 6.

Seventeenth-century doctor William Butler was right about strawberries in the seventeenth century, and today as well: "Doubtless God could have made a better berry, but doubtless God never did." Red, ripe, and redolent, strawberries, buried in this cake, make a summer-tasting dish ideal for the harvesting time.

Strawberry Honeydew Cheese Pie

CRUST:

1   C unbleached all-purpose flour
½   t salt
⅓   C shortening
2   T lime juice
2   T cold water

FILLING:

3   oz. cream cheese, softened
2   T confectioners' sugar
1   C ripe strawberries
½   C water
½   C sugar
2   T cornstarch
⅛   t salt
2   T sweet butter
    grated rind of 1 lime
3   C fresh honeydew balls, drained

1. For crust, mix flour and salt. Cut in shortening. Stir in lime juice and water one T at a time until dough forms a ball. Roll out dough and place in 9-inch pie plate. Pierce with fork. Bake at 450 degrees F. for 7–9 minutes or until lightly toasted. Cool.

2. For filling, blend cream cheese and sugar. Spread over bottom of crust.

3. Crush strawberries partially and combine with water. Simmer 5 minutes and press through sieve. Discard residue.

4. Blend sugar, cornstarch, and salt. Stir into strawberry mixture. Cook over medium heat, stirring constantly until mixture boils. Continue cooking and stirring over low heat 2 minutes.

5. Remove from heat and stir in butter and lime peel. Cool until lukewarm.

6. Place honeydew balls on top of cheese. Spoon strawberry glaze over them. Cool. Chill. Serves 6.

One of the most felicitous combinations of fresh fruits is a bite of succulent honeydew melon coated with lime juice. Few tastes brighten up the world as well as this. This recipe harbors the sparkling honeydew-lime taste along with the friendly strawberry flavor.

Strawberry Sour Cream Cheesecake

CRUST:
- 1 C graham cracker crumbs
- 3 T sweet butter, melted

FILLING:
- 12 oz. cream cheese, softened
- 2 large eggs, slightly beaten
- ½ C sugar
- ½ t vanilla extract

TOPPING:
- 2 C sour cream
- ¼ C sugar
- ¼ C ground toasted blanched almonds
- whole strawberries

GLAZE:
- ¼ C red currant jelly
- 1 T water

1. For crust, mix crumbs with butter. Press onto bottom and up side of 8-inch springform pan. Bake at 450 degrees F. for 4 minutes or until set. Cool.

2. For filling, beat cheese until smooth and light.

3. Beat in eggs one at a time. Gradually add sugar and vanilla.

4. Pour into crust and bake at 350 degrees F. for 20 minutes.

5. For topping, blend sour cream, sugar, and almonds. Spread evenly over top of cake.

6. Return cake to oven for 5–7 minutes or until set. Cool. Chill.

7. Before serving, decoratively place whole prepared strawberries on top of cake.

8. For glaze, mix currant jelly and water and melt over medium heat. Pour over strawberries. Serves 10.

Besides the taste, this cake appeals because of its four layers of interest. It's a relatively easy cake to prepare for such an inviting result, especially for the piquant currant glaze that glistens the strawberries to their reddest.

Tangerine Mandarin Orange Cheesecake

CRUST:
½ C unbleached all-purpose
   flour
   dash of salt
   grated rind of 1 orange
4 T sweet butter

FILLING:
6 oz. tangerine juice
   concentrate, thawed
2 large eggs, separated
8 oz. Neuchatel cheese,
   softened
⅓ C unbleached all-purpose
   flour
½ C sugar
1 C heavy cream, whipped

GLAZE:
   Mandarin oranges, 11 oz. can
   (reserve juice)
¼ C orange juice
2 T sugar
   dash of salt
1 T cornstarch dissolved in 1 T
   water

1. For crust, combine flour, salt, and rind. Cut in butter. Chill. Press onto bottom and over rim joint of an 8-inch springform pan. Bake at 450 degrees F. for 4 minutes or until lightly toasted. Cool.

2. For filling, place concentrate, egg yolks, cheese, flour, and sugar in blender and whirl until light. Pour into large bowl.

3. Fold in whipped cream. Beat egg whites until stiff and fold into mixture.

4. Pour into crust. Bake at 325 degrees F. for 40–50 minutes or until center is set. Top turns dark golden brown. Cool. To maintain the cake height, turn off the heat and leave the cake inside for thirty minutes, if the top is not too dark.

5. For glaze, drain oranges, reserve juice and set both aside. To reserved juice in saucepan add orange juice, sugar, and salt. Heat. Mix cornstarch in water and add to juices. Stirring, heat slowly until thickened and glossy. Cool.

6. Remove side of pan from cake. Arrange oranges decoratively around edge of cake.

7. Brush glaze over entire top of cake. Chill 2 hours. Serves 10.

The Mandarin orange is a kind of tangerine, and the tangerine, in turn, is a kind of orange. The tastes here parallel each other. Tangerine concentrate offers a subtle orangy flavor to this airy smallish cake. Don't remove the cake too soon from the oven before it has set; if you do, it will fall too much. Overlapping the Mandarin oranges in a circle on top against the mahogany-colored rim makes an attractive setting for a fall season table.

Tapioca Cheesecake

CRUST:
¾ C mint sandwich cookie
     crumbs, whirled in blender
     sweet butter for pan

FILLING:
1 lb. cream cheese, softened
2 large eggs, separated
2 T instant tapioca
½ C all-purpose cream
½ C sugar
½ t salt
1 t vanilla extract

1. For crust, press half of crumbs on bottom and up side of well buttered 8-inch springform pan. Reserve the rest of the crumbs for the topping.
2. For filling, beat the cheese and egg yolks together until smooth and creamy. Beat whites until stiff but not dry. Set aside.
3. Sprinkle tapioca over cream for 5 minutes to soften.
4. Add sugar and salt to cheese mixture. Blend in cream mixture, breaking up tapioca. Gradually, bring the mixture to a full boil and cook for 1–2 minutes, stirring constantly.
5. Remove from heat and fold in whites. Stir in vanilla. Pour into crust. Cool. Chill until set. Sprinkle remaining crumbs on top. Serves 6–8.

Tapioca is an extract from the manioc, a tropical plant, and, as a nearly pure high quality starch, it is digested easily. Tapioca thickens well and allows a cooked cheesecake to be made in minutes instead of hours. This cake is simple-tasting and simple-making.

Tofu Pineapple Cheesecake

CRUST:
⅔ C coconut
⅔ C toasted wheat germ
3 T light brown sugar
1 t allspice
¼ C sweet butter, melted

FILLING:
4 eggs
¾ C honey
3 C fresh tofu
2 t vanilla extract
1 C light cream
1 T fresh lemon juice
¼ t almond extract

TOPPING:
8 oz. crushed pineapple
2 T orange juice
1 T cornstarch

1. For crust, mix together coconut, wheat germ, brown sugar, and allspice. Stir in butter. Press mixture onto bottom and up side of 9-inch springform pan. Bake at 450 degrees F. for 4 minutes or until set. Cool.

2. For filling, place eggs, honey, tofu, vanilla, cream, lemon juice, and almond in a blender and whirl until smooth.

3. Pour into crust.

4. Bake at 325 degrees F. for 45 minutes or until center is set. Cool. Remove rim of pan.

5. For topping, combine pineapple, orange juice, and cornstarch in a saucepan. Stirring constantly, cook over medium heat until slightly thickened. Cool slightly. Spread over cake. Chill completely. Serves 10–12.

This is a mock cheesecake because, strictly speaking, tofu is not a cheese. It is a curd made from coagulating soybean "milk," but it has a cheese-like texture. Very rich in protein and containing all eight essential amino acids, tofu is one of the oldest prepared foods in the world, having originated two thousand years ago in China. It doesn't keep long, and must be purchased fresh, so use it right away. Some tofu "cheesecake" recipes are heavy on the bland bean curd taste. Not this one.

Two-layer Cheesecake

CRUST:
1 C chocolate wafer crumbs
¼ C sweet butter, melted

FILLING:
First layer
2 oz. unsweetened chocolate, melted
2 large eggs
8 oz. cream cheese, softened
1 t instant coffee granules
1 T water
½ C sugar, divided

Second layer
2 T fresh lemon juice
2 large eggs, separated
8 oz. cream cheese, softened
⅓ C sugar
1 T unflavored gelatin
¼ C cold water

GLAZE:
⅓ C apricot jam, strained
2 t honey
2 T water

1. For crust, mix crumbs with butter. Press onto bottom and up side of 8-inch springform pan. The side crust should rise evenly only 1 inch.
2. For filling, melt the chocolate over hot water.
3. Beat eggs into cheese.
4. Dissolve coffee into water.
5. Stir ¼ C sugar into the melted chocolate. Add the coffee mixture.
6. Stir in ¼ C sugar into the cheese mixture. Then combine the chocolate and cheese mixtures.
7. Pour into crust. Bake at 325 degrees F. for 25–30 minutes or until center is set. Remove from oven and cool.
8. For second layer, blend lemon juice and egg yolks into cheese.
9. Beat egg whites until soft peaks form. Gradually add sugar and beat until stiff.
10. Pour gelatin over water and dissolve over low heat, stirring constantly. Stir well into cheese mixture.
11. Immediately fold meringue into cheese mixture. Pour and smooth mixture gently onto top of chocolate layer in springform pan. Refrigerate to set the gelatin.
12. For glaze, strain the apricot jam. Add honey and water, and simmer over low heat until blended and slightly thickened. Cool slightly.
13. Remove side of springform pan. Carefully spread glaze over top of cake. With extra glaze, dribble over side of cake. Serves 12.

Once cut, this cake makes a striking display of its colors. The midnight dark crust, underlying the dark chocolate, underlying the snow-white top layer—all are offset by the luscious-looking golden apricot glaze. The cake is designed for contrasts in colors, tastes, and textures. The thick coffee-hinting chocolate is balanced by the cool, light, lemon top layer. This one takes some time to prepare, but a two-layer cheesecake, a rarity, is worth the effort for special occasions.

Yogurt Cheesecake

1 C graham cracker crumbs
3 T sweet butter, melted

FILLING:
4 large eggs
2 C cottage cheese, sieved
½ C sugar
½ t salt
1 t fresh lemon juice
¼ t grated fresh nutmeg

TOPPING:
1½ C plain yogurt
2 T sugar
½ t vanilla extract

1. For crust, mix crumbs and butter. Press onto bottom and up side of 8-inch springform pan. Bake at 450 degrees F. for 4 minutes or until set. Cool.
2. For filling, beat eggs and cheese until smooth and light.
3. Blend in sugar, salt, and lemon juice.
4. Pour into crust. Grate on nutmeg.
5. Bake at 350 degrees F. for 20 minutes or until nearly set.
6. For topping, blend yogurt, sugar, and vanilla. Pour over cheese mixture. Return to oven for 10–15 minutes or until set. Cool. Chill. Serves 6–8.

Mixing fruit with the yogurt adds a colorful, tasty dimension to the topping. If you make your own yogurt, adding sweetened fruit is easy. Or stir up one of the commercial fruit yogurts, such as raspberry, blueberry, or strawberry, and spread this on top.

THE SAVORIES

Quiches and Appetizers

Artichoke Heart Quiche

CRUST:
1 C unbleached all-purpose
   flour
½ t salt
2 T sweet butter
3 T shortening
2–3 T cold water

FILLING:
9 oz. package frozen
   artichoke hearts, cooked
2 thin slices baked ham
1½ C shredded Swiss cheese
3 large eggs, slightly beaten
½ t salt
   dash of white pepper
1½ C half-and-half cream
   paprika

1. For crust, mix flour and salt. Cut in butter and shortening. Stir in water one T at a time until dough forms a ball. Adding flour when necessary, roll out and place in 9-inch quiche pan. Pierce with fork. Bake at 450 degrees F. for 7–9 minutes or until lightly toasted. Cool.

2. For filling, prepare artichoke hearts and set aside.

3. Arrange ham slices to cover crust completely.

4. Spread on cheese.

5. Combine eggs, salt, white pepper, and half-and-half. Pour over cheese.

6. Arrange artichoke hearts decoratively in a circle on top of the filling. Sprinkle lightly with paprika.

7. Bake at 350 degrees F. for 25–30 minutes or until center is set. Don't overcook.

8. Remove from pan. Cool 3–4 minutes. Slice with sharp knife to cut ham. Serves 6.

The sweet taste of unadorned artichoke hearts makes a special treat for this quiche. The added bonus is utter simplicity and quick preparation for an elegant taste. Artichoke hearts are a versatile delicacy and may be used cold in salads or baked stuffed with crabmeat or a seasoned bread mixture. The so-called Jerusalem artichoke is a tuber related to the sunflower family and is not a thistle, as is the better known globe or French artichoke used in this dish.

Asparagus Quiche

CRUST:
1 C unbleached all-purpose
    flour
½ t salt
2 T sweet butter
3 T shortening
4 T cold milk

FILLING:
1 lb. fresh slender asparagus
    spears
1 C shredded mild Cheddar
    cheese
¾ C milk
¾ C light cream
⅓ C diced scallions
1 t salt
¼ t allspice
    dash of white pepper
3 large eggs, slightly beaten

1. For crust, mix flour and salt. Cut in butter and shortening. Stir in milk one T at a time until dough forms a ball. Roll out and place in 9-inch quiche pan. Pierce with fork. Bake at 450 degrees F. for 7–9 minutes or until lightly toasted. Cool.

2. For filling, steam asparagus until slightly tender on the stems (about 10–12 minutes). Don't overcook.

3. Sprinkle ¾ of the cheese into the crust.

4. Arrange asparagus decoratively over cheese.

5. Blend milk, cream, scallions, salt, allspice, and pepper in saucepan. Simmer 1 minute. Remove from heat.

6. Slowly stir cream mixture into eggs. Pour onto cheese.

7. Sprinkle remaining cheese on top.

8. Bake at 350 degrees F. for 20–25 minutes or until set. Serves 6.

Always look for the thin stalks of asparagus, the youngest and most tender. The fat ones you should peel and trim. The best possible asparagus are the wild ones that sprout in fields and along roadsides in spring. They look exactly like the market variety, but their taste is brighter. Rush them home and, if you can resist steaming them and serving them with a homemade hollandaise sauce, prepare them for this quiche, the next best way to eat what the ancient Romans considered the royalty of vegetables.

Bacon and Tomato Quiche

CRUST:
1 C unbleached all-purpose
   flour
½ t salt
⅓ C shortening
4 T cold water

FILLING:
8 rashers lean bacon
2 large tomatoes, de-seeded
1 C shredded sharp Cheddar
   cheese
8 oz. cream cheese, softened
¾ C light cream

1. For crust, mix flour and salt. Cut in shortening. Stir in water one T at a time until dough forms a ball. Roll out and place in 9-inch quiche pan. Pierce with fork. Bake at 450 degrees F. for 7–9 minutes or until lightly toasted. Cool.

2. For filling, broil bacon, reserving fat. Set both aside.

3. Slice tomatoes ½-inch thick. Remove seeds and liquid with small spoon. Set aside.

4. Sprinkle Cheddar on bottom of crust. Place tomato slices on top of Cheddar. Lay strips of bacon on top of tomatoes.

5. Beat cream cheese until light. Pour in cream and bacon fat and mix thoroughly. Pour this mixture over tomatoes.

6. Bake at 350 degrees F. for about 30 minutes or until cheese mixture is set. Remove pan side and serve immediately. Serves 5–6.

Particularly good with plump, garden-fresh beefsteak tomatoes, this quiche has no eggs. It is simple and straightforward, but the combination of bacon and tomato, as nearly everyone knows from sandwiches, is difficult to top. The added combination of Cheddar and tomato makes this quiche all the more appealing. Salt from the bacon and cheese eliminates the need to add more. This recipe produces a thin quiche, and is therefore better in tandem with a larger luncheon menu.

Beer and Sauerkraut Quiche

CRUST:

1 C unbleached all-purpose flour
½ t salt
3 T sweet butter
2 T shortening
1 egg yolk
2–3 T cold milk

FILLING:

8 rashers lean bacon, cooked crisp and crumbled
2 C grated Swiss cheese
1 T unbleached all-purpose flour
2 T sweet butter
¼ C minced onion
1 C rinsed and drained sauerkraut
3 large eggs, slightly beaten
¾ C beer
¼ C milk
dash of hot sauce
½ t salt
⅛ t dry mustard

1. For crust, mix flour and salt. Cut in butter and shortening. Stir in egg yolk and then milk one T at a time. Form a ball. Chill before rolling out and placing in 9-inch quiche pan. Pierce with fork. Bake at 450 degrees F. for 7–9 minutes or until lightly toasted. Cool.
2. For filling, toss together half of crumbled bacon, half of cheese, and flour. Sprinkle evenly over pastry shell. Add rest of cheese.
3. Melt butter in skillet. Add onion and sauté until tender, not brown.
4. Add sauerkraut and cook a few minutes.
5. Arrange evenly over cheese in crust.
6. Sprinkle with remaining crumbled bacon.
7. Beat together eggs, beer, milk, hot sauce, salt, and mustard. Pour over cheese mixture.
8. Bake at 350 degrees F. for 30–35 minutes or until set and toasted. Cool slightly before serving. Serves 6.

Based on a recipe served at the Breezemere Farm in the craggy seacoast village of South Brooksville, Maine, this unusual but toothsome dish appeals far more to the tongue's taste than it may to the mind's eye. Perfect for an appetizer. Since sauerkraut is made with heavy doses of salt, rinse and drain it before preparing this or any similar recipe.

Black Bean and Rice Quiche

CRUST:
1 C unbleached all-purpose
   flour
½ t salt
⅓ C shortening
3 T grated Parmesan cheese
4 T cold water

FILLING:
½ C black beans, cooked
¾ C rice, cooked
2 small onions, diced
1 T olive oil
1 C grated Cheddar cheese
2 large eggs, beaten
½ C milk
¼ C sour cream
½ t salt
⅛ t white pepper
¼ t cumin

1. For crust, mix flour and salt. Cut in shortening. Mix in Parmesan. Stir in water one T at a time until dough forms a ball. Roll out and place in 9-inch quiche pan. Pierce with fork. Bake at 450 degrees F. for 7–9 minutes or until lightly toasted. Cool.
2. For filling, cook beans and rice. Combine and set aside.
3. Sauté onions in olive oil until transparent, not brown.
4. Mix Cheddar into beans and rice. Add onions and leftover oil from skillet.
5. Combine eggs, milk, sour cream, salt, pepper, and cumin. Pour into bean mixture and blend.
6. Pour mixture into crust. Bake at 350 degrees F. for 25 minutes or until top of rice is slightly toasted. Don't overbake. Serve hot. Serves 6.

This earthy dish contains one of the most basic food combinations of all—beans and rice. They complement each other in many ways, including taste, texture, nutrition, and aesthetics. Black beans and cumin give this quiche a Mexican touch. Black beans are best soaked overnight and then cooked a couple of hours. They are especially attractive set against white rice, although brown rice works satisfactorily with this, too.

Brussels Sprouts and Ham Quiche

CRUST:
- 1 C unbleached all-purpose flour
- ½ t salt
- ⅓ C shortening
- 4 T cold water

FILLING:
- ¾ lb. small fresh Brussels sprouts, cooked thoroughly
- 1 C baked ham, thinly sliced
- 1 C plain yogurt
- ⅔ C evaporated milk
- ½ t salt
- ¼ t white pepper
- ¼ t freshly grated nutmeg
- 3 eggs, well beaten
- 1 C grated Cheddar cheese
- ⅓ C grated Parmesan cheese

1. For crust, mix flour and salt. Cut in shortening. Stir in water one T at a time until dough forms a ball. Roll out and place in 9-inch quiche pan. Pierce with fork. Bake at 450 degrees F. for 7–9 minutes or until lightly toasted. Cool.

2. For filling, slice sprouts lengthwise in half. Set aside.

3. Cut ham into half-a-finger-sized sections. Set aside.

4. Mix yogurt, milk, salt, pepper, and nutmeg. Blend in eggs.

5. Place ham pieces in crust. Sprinkle on Cheddar and then Parmesan cheeses.

6. Pour on egg mixture. Carefully place sprout halves decoratively in close-knit circles on top.

7. Bake at 350 degrees F. for 40 minutes or until slightly toasted. Remove pan side. Serves 6.

Brussels sprouts are miniature cabbages. They have a more delicate flavor than their full-blown relatives. For this dish the sprouts should be cooked more, for ease of cutting, than they would be if they were to be served alone. Place a few bread cubes in the pot while cooking to extract some of the cabbage-y odors. The sprouts grow on the stalk in the axils of the large leathery silver-grey leaves. They are true sprouts, and contain all the good nutrients and rounded flavor that you expect from sprouts.

Cheese Puffs

2 T sweet butter
3½ T unbleached all-purpose flour
4 T shredded Cheddar cheese
¼ t salt
few grains cayenne
2 large egg whites, stiffly beaten

1. Melt butter. Stir in flour until well blended.
2. Remove from heat. Stir in cheese, salt, and cayenne.
3. Fold in egg whites.
4. To make puffs, drop batter from a teaspoon one inch apart onto a greased baking sheet.
5. Bake at 350 degrees F. for 10–12 minutes or until golden and set. Makes 12–16.

These soufflé-like, bite-sized puffs are addictive, and very quick to make. Don't overbake them, but bake them just enough so that they melt like cheese air in your mouth.

Cheese Soufflé

3 T sweet butter
3 T unbleached all-purpose
   flour
1 C milk
1 C grated sharp Cheddar
   cheese
3 large eggs, separated
½ t salt
⅛ t paprika
1 T Cognac
1 T grated Parmesan

1. In large skillet, melt butter. Whisk in flour.
2. Pour in ⅓ C milk and blend with the butter mixture. Add rest of milk. Heat over medium-low temperature.
3. Sprinkle in Cheddar and stir to melt completely.
4. Beat egg yolks well, and gradually add to Cheddar mixture, stirring constantly.
5. Add salt and paprika. Simmer to thicken. Transfer to mixing bowl.
6. Beat whites until stiff but not dry. Fold whites into Cheddar mixture. Stir in Cognac. Pour into buttered 1½-quart dish. Smooth top. To make top-knot cap, gouge a 1-inch deep, 1-inch wide edge around soufflé.
7. Sprinkle on Parmesan. Bake at 350 degrees F. for 30 minutes or until well toasted and set. Serve immediately. Serves 2–4.

A good cheese soufflé is easy to make if you proceed slowly and methodically, keeping the burner temperatures low. Some variations you might try are: an extra egg white to give more lift (with corresponding reduction in cheese concentration); Gruyère in place of Cheddar; beer instead of Cognac; dry mustard for paprika.

Chick Pea and Lentil Quiche

CRUST:
- 1 C unbleached all-purpose flour
- ½ t salt
- ⅓ C shortening
- 1 T chopped chives
- 4 T cold water

FILLING:
- ½ C lentils, cooked
- ½ C rice, cooked
- 1 garlic clove, diced
- 1 small onion, diced
- 1 T olive oil
- 1 C grated Cheddar cheese
- 2 C cooked chick peas (or 1-lb.-4-oz. can)
- 1 T chopped parsley
- ½ t salt
- ¼ t pepper
- 1 large pimento, sliced
- 3 large eggs
- 1 C light cream

1. For crust, mix flour and salt. Cut in shortening. Stir in chives. Stir in water one T at a time until dough forms a ball. Roll out and place in high-sided 9-inch quiche pan. Pierce with fork. Bake at 450 degrees F. for 7–9 minutes or until lightly toasted. Cool.

2. For filling, cook lentils and rice. Sauté garlic and onion in olive oil until transparent, not brown.

3. Spread cheese on bottom of crust.

4. Mix chick peas, parsley, salt, pepper, and pimento in large bowl. Mix in lentils and rice. Pour over cheese.

5. Mix eggs and cream. Pour over chick pea mixture. Bake at 350 degrees F. for 40 minutes or until center is set and very lightly toasted. Serve hot. Serves 6–8.

The combination of chick peas (or garbanzos) and lentils makes a hearty dish. This recipe produces a large, filling pie that is as robust reheated as the first time around.

Chicken Curry Cheese Pie

CRUST:

1   C unbleached all-purpose
      flour
½   t salt
⅓   C shortening
4   T cold water

FILLING:

1   medium-sized chicken breast,
      split, skinned, poached,
      shredded
1   T olive oil
1   medium-sized onion, sliced
2   large eggs, slightly beaten
1   C light cream
⅓   C plain yogurt
½   t salt
⅛   t white pepper
½   t ground turmeric
¼   t ground coriander
      dash of cloves
½   t ground cumin
1   t grated fresh gingerroot
4   oz. cream cheese, softened
      paprika

1. For crust, mix flour and salt. Cut in shortening. Stir in water one T at a time until dough forms a ball. Roll out and place in 9-inch pie plate. Pierce with fork. Bake at 450 degrees F. for 7–9 minutes or until lightly toasted. Cool.

2. For filling, prepare chicken and set aside.

3. In oil, sauté onion until transparent, not brown.

4. In large mixing bowl, combine eggs, cream, yogurt, salt, pepper, turmeric, coriander, cloves, cumin, and gingerroot.

5. Beat cream cheese with wooden spoon until it is pasty. Add to egg mixture. Blend in the cheese with a large whisk so that the cheese is broken into small particles.

6. Add the chicken to the cheese mixture and stir. Pour into crust. Sprinkle on paprika decoratively.

7. Bake at 350 degrees F. for 30 minutes or until lightly toasted and center is set. Serves 6.

Curry is a condiment that may have more than a dozen ingredients. The best curries are made from fresh rather than dry ingredients, and therefore must be made frequently. Nevertheless, this recipe has the familiar but mild curry spark. Most curries have turmeric, cumin, and gingerroot as their foundation, with other spices added according to taste. This savory pie is rich and creamy, with a relatively understated tang and piquancy that add an East Indian–Oriental dimension to the taste.

Chicken Quiche

CRUST:

1 C unbleached all-purpose
  flour
½ t salt
2 T sweet butter
3 T shortening
1 egg yolk
3–4 T cold water

FILLING:

1 chicken breast, split,
  cooked, shredded (about
  1¼ C)
1½ C (6 oz.) shredded Swiss
  cheese
3 large eggs
¾ C light cream
¾ C milk
½ t salt
  dash of white pepper
3 T grated Parmesan cheese

1. For crust, mix flour and salt. Cut in butter and shortening. Stir in egg yolk and then cold water one T at a time until dough forms a ball. Chill. Roll out and place in 9-inch quiche pan. Pierce with fork. Bake at 450 degrees F. for 7–9 minutes or until lightly toasted. Cool.

2. For filling, spread chicken on bottom of crust in pan. Sprinkle on Swiss cheese.

3. In separate bowl beat eggs. Blend in cream and milk. Add salt and pepper. Pour over the cheese and chicken.

4. Sprinkle on Parmesan cheese.

5. Bake at 350 degrees F. for about 30 minutes or until center is set. The top should have toasted spots.

6. Let stand for 5 minutes before slicing and serving. Serves 6.

If you cook the chicken breast in a pot of water, afterward the broth may be used as a base for a good nourishing soup. The quiche itself comes out relatively thin in a nine-inch pan; an eight-inch pan makes it slightly thicker. It's a mild-tasting dish, probably best for a Sunday brunch along with a small green salad, crusty warm sourdough French bread, and fresh melons or cold peaches and cream.

Chili Bean Pie

CRUST:

1	C masa harina
½	t salt
⅓	C shortening
1¼	C water

FILLING:

1	medium-sized onion, diced
1	clove garlic, minced
1	T corn oil
1½	C cooked red kidney beans
¾	lb. cooked shredded beef
4	oz. cooked green chilis, chopped
1	C crushed tomatoes
1	T tomato paste
2	t fresh chili powder
1	t salt
⅛	t freshly ground black pepper
½	t cumin
1	C shredded Monterey Jack cheese

1. For crust, mix masa harina and salt. Beat in shortening. Stir in water a little at a time until dough is pourable. Spread in a 12 × 8 × 2-inch greased baking dish.

2. For filling, sauté onion and garlic in oil until transparent, not brown.

3. Combine in saucepan onion, garlic, beans, beef, chilis, tomatoes, tomato paste.

4. Stir in chili powder, salt, pepper, and cumin. Simmer covered 20 minutes.

5. Pour into crust. Sprinkle on cheese. Bake at 350 degrees F. for 30 minutes or until cheese is lightly toasted. Serves 6.

Fine yellow cornmeal may be used in place of the traditional Mexican masa harina when the latter is unavailable. If you use fresh green chilis rather than the prepared canned ones, it's better to roast and peel them first. Pierce the chilis with a fork, place them on a baking sheet, and roast them under a broiler for a few minutes, turning frequently. Cover with a damp cloth to steam them, and then peel off the blistered skin. Growers of chilis rate the heat of chili peppers from 1 to 120. The jalapeno registers a 15, and we think that one is hot!

Corn Cheese Pie

CRUST:

1 C unbleached all-purpose flour
2 T toasted wheat germ
½ t salt
⅓ C shortening
4 T cold water

FILLING:

½ C plain yogurt
¾ C light cream
2 large eggs, slightly beaten
½ t salt
¼ t white pepper
⅓ C green pepper, de-seeded, de-stemmed, finely chopped
1 small onion, diced
3 T chopped pimento
2 T chopped parsley
2 C fresh corn, de-cobbed, cooked
   pinch of fresh sage
⅓ C grated Cheddar cheese

1. For crust, mix flour, wheat germ, and salt. Cut in shortening. Stir in water one T at a time until dough forms a ball. Roll out and place in 9-inch pie plate. Pierce with fork. Bake at 450 degrees F. for 7–9 minutes or until lightly toasted. Cool.
2. For filling, mix yogurt, cream, and eggs together well.
3. Stir in salt, white pepper, green pepper, onion, pimento, parsley, corn, and sage. Pour into crust.
4. Sprinkle with cheese.
5. Bake at 350 degrees F. for 30 minutes or until center is set.
Serves 6.

Fresh corn on the cob, such as the butter and sugar variety, is sweet immediately after picking. Within an hour or so, the natural sugar turns to starch, so get it freshly picked if you can. Cook it briefly (about three to four minutes). The yogurt gives this dish a slightly tart undertaste; the green, yellow, and red color makes this a lively-looking, confetti kind of dish.

Corn Sausage Cheese Pie

  1   C unbleached all-purpose
      flour
  ½   t salt
  ⅓   C shortening
  4   T cold water

FILLING:
  6   sausage links, cooked, cut
      into pieces
  ½   C grated Swiss cheese
  ½   C buttermilk
  1   C light cream
  1½ C creamed corn
  1   t salt
      pepper to taste
  2   T Parmesan cheese

1. For crust, mix flour and salt. Cut in shortening. Stir in water one T at a time until dough forms a ball. Chill while cooking sausages. Roll out and place in 9-inch pie plate. Pierce with fork. Bake at 450 degrees F. for 7–9 minutes or until lightly toasted. Cool.

2. For filling, place sausage pieces in crust. Sprinkle with Swiss cheese.

3. Mix buttermilk, cream, corn, salt, and pepper. Pour over sausage and cheese.

4. Sprinkle with Parmesan cheese.

5. Bake at 350 degrees F. for 30 minutes or until center is set. Serves 6.

In off-corn season, when you long for the all-American vegetable, this dish brings back at least some summer taste in winter. A good spicy sausage without nitrites and other additives is preferred, and, of course, when summer corn arrives, fresh kernels scraped off the cobs and put in a light cream sauce make the best taste.

Crab and Avocado Quiche

CRUST:

1 C unbleached all-purpose
   flour
½ t salt
⅓ C shortening
4 T cold water

FILLING:

½ lb. fresh crabmeat
1 pimento, sliced
1 avocado
1 medium-sized onion, diced
1 T olive oil
2 large eggs
⅔ C ricotta
½ C light cream
½ t mustard
½ t salt
   dash of white pepper

1. For crust, mix flour and salt. Cut in shortening. Stir in water one T at a time until dough forms a ball. Roll out and place in 9-inch quiche pan. Pierce with fork. Bake at 450 degrees F. for 7–9 minutes or until lightly toasted. Cool.

2. For filling, mix crabmeat and pimento. Spread on crust.

3. Peel avocado and remove pit. Slice quarter-inch sections lengthwise and place over crabmeat.

4. Sauté onion in olive oil until transparent, not brown. Spread over avocado.

5. Beat eggs slightly. Stir in ricotta and cream. Blend in mustard, salt, and pepper. Pour over crabmeat.

6. Bake at 350 degrees F. for 35 minutes or until lightly toasted. Serves 6.

Crabmeat is the basis for an elegant dish. Coupled with buttery, rich avocado slices, this quiche assumes a central role in a warm summer luncheon, with popovers, perhaps a nice dry white wine, and peach sherbet.

Eggplant Quiche

CRUST:

1 C unbleached all-purpose
   flour
½ t salt
⅓ C shortening
4 T cold water

FILLING:

2 medium-sized white onions,
   diced
  olive oil
1 medium-sized eggplant,
   peeled and chopped
4 t pesto
4 large tomatoes, chopped
¾ t oregano
½ t salt
⅛ t black pepper
2 t tomato paste
3 large eggs
1 egg yolk
¼ C grated Parmesan cheese
½ C plain yogurt
½ C light cream

1. For crust, mix flour and salt. Cut in shortening. Stir in water one T at a time until dough forms a ball. Roll out and place in 9-inch quiche pan. Pierce with fork. Bake at 450 degrees F. for 7–9 minutes or until lightly toasted. Cool.

2. For filling, sauté onions in 2 T olive oil until transparent, not brown.

3. Add eggplant and only enough oil so as not to scorch. Cook until tender and reduced in size, stirring as needed.

4. Stir in pesto. Then add tomatoes, oregano, salt, pepper, and tomato paste. Mix well. Cook until slightly thickened. Place in crust.

5. In separate bowl beat eggs and yolk until mixed. Add Parmesan, yogurt, and cream. Blend.

6. Pour egg mixture over eggplant mixture.

7. Bake at 350 degrees F. for 30 minutes or until set. Serves 6–8.

The large purple plant shaped like an egg, like many other versatile plants, was once thought to cause madness if eaten. Those who now know better grow their own eggplant, so they can pick them fresh and within an hour slice, bread, and sauté them in olive oil for a true delight. For store-bought eggplants, however, this quiche makes good use of ones that aren't fresh but still have the mild taste and texture that go so well with tomatoes and cheese. A basic pesto to have on hand for this and other recipes is: about an equal amount of crushed or minced fresh basil leaves and parsley, some minced garlic cloves, and enough olive oil to make a paste. Crushed pine nuts and Parmesan cheese may also be added.

Feta Cheese Pie

CRUST:

20 phyllo sheets
¼   C sweet butter, melted, and
     butter for dish

FILLING:

1   lb. feta cheese
1   lb. ricotta
3   large eggs, slightly beaten
½   C light cream
2   T unbleached all-purpose
     flour
2   T chopped parsley
½   t mace

1. For crust, butter 12 × 8 × 2-inch glass baking dish. Place in it 10 phyllo sheets, brushing each with melted butter.

2. For filling, soak salty feta in water and drain. Blend feta and ricotta.

3. Beat in eggs one at a time. Add cream.

4. Mix in flour, parsley, and mace.

5. Spread the cheese mixture on the phyllo crust. Then cover with the 10 remaining sheets, brushing each with melted butter. Tuck the edges of the crust into the dish sides. Sprinkle crust with water.

6. Score the top halfway through the phyllo into serving-sized sections.

7. Bake at 350 degrees F. for 30 minutes. Cool slightly before cutting. Serves 4–6.

This Greek cheese pie is called a *tyropita*. A phyllo crust is used for many Greek and Middle Eastern dishes. Most likely you'll find the sheets frozen (phyllo needs to be too thin for home preparation). Work fast with them. Keep what sheets you're not using immediately wrapped in a damp towel so they won't dry and become useless. Feta is a goat cheese preserved in brine. It is a mild chunky cheese, best known in Greek salads, but used effectively here, too.

Fondue

1 clove garlic
1 lb. finely grated Gruyère cheese
1 T unbleached all-purpose flour
1 C dry white wine
⅛ t salt
dash of white pepper
⅛ t freshly ground nutmeg
⅓ C Kirsch
cubed French bread

1. Rub a heavy saucepan with garlic clove. Discard clove.
2. Mix cheese with flour.
3. Bring wine nearly to boil in saucepan.
4. Add cheese and stir constantly with whisk or fork until dissolved. Keep stirring.
5. Add salt, pepper, and nutmeg.
6. At the threshold of the boiling point, add Kirsch and blend quickly. Serve immediately. Keep fondue warm over alcohol lamp or in fondue pot.
7. Serve cubed French bread on the side with fondue forks for dipping. Serves 3–4.

Fondue is the classic Swiss dish. It may be successfully varied with Emmenthaler cheese and another flavoring, such as Cognac. A good Graves wine works well. The bread should be cut in bite-sized, one-inch cubes, each with a crusty side. The fork is best pierced through one of the soft sides to the crust.

Fritters

¼   **C diced onion**
1   **T olive oil**
½   **C unbleached all-purpose**
      flour
⅛   **t salt**
1   **large egg, separated**
½   **C beer**
2   **drops prepared hot sauce**
½   **C Cheddar, diced**
      oil for deep frying

1. Sauté onion in oil until transparent, not brown. Set aside with its oil.
2. Mix flour and salt.
3. Mix egg yolk with beer and hot sauce. Stir into flour mixture.
4. Stir in onion with its oil. Allow batter to rest 1 hour.
5. Beat egg white until stiff but not dry. Fold into batter. Fold Cheddar into batter.
6. Heat oil to 375 degrees F. Drop batter by teaspoons into oil and deep fry until well toasted. Drain on absorbant paper and serve immediately. Makes 30.

Fritters may be made of just about any small-sized food. The Italians, in fact, call these *fritto misto*, meaning mixed fritters. Some plain fritters, such as corn fritters, are delicious served hot and doused with sweet butter and authentic maple syrup. Others, such as these cheese fritters (they may be made successfully with Gruyère, too) are best merely eaten as is but hot. So prepare them right before you plan to serve them.

Gingered Cheese Balls

1   C grated Cheddar cheese
3   T unbleached all-purpose
    flour
¼   t salt
¼   t dry mustard
¾   t grated fresh gingerroot
2   large egg whites, beaten
⅔   C bread crumbs
    corn oil for deep frying

1. Mix cheese, flour, salt, mustard, and gingerroot.
2. Blend in egg whites.
3. Form teaspoon-sized balls of mixture and coat them with bread crumbs. Set aside on plate for 15–20 minutes.
4. Heat oil to 365 degrees F. Deep fry the cheese balls, a few at a time, for about 15 seconds or until well toasted on all sides. Makes about 20.

These light, pungent appetizers may be served warm or cold. Ginger is extremely versatile and may be used to inspire nearly any food from pears to waffles. Rubbing gingerroot rather than garlic on steaks and roasts makes a refreshing detour, as does scattering a little grated fresh gingerroot on vegetables like beets and beans. Any respectable curry must include ginger, and nuggets of crystallized gingerroot in homemade vanilla ice cream offer a delightful surprise. Ginger doesn't stop here. Drinking ginger tea stimulates the appetite, while sliced ginger in soups zings up the aroma and taste. Imagination is the only limit for a judicious use of ginger.

Gnocchi Verdi

8   oz. ricotta
10   oz. fresh spinach
⅓   C grated Parmesan cheese
1   egg, slightly beaten
¼   t nutmeg
     flour as needed
¼   C sweet butter, melted

1. Drain ricotta and press out all water.
2. Cook spinach. Drain and press out all water. Chop finely.
3. Blend ricotta, Parmesan, spinach, egg, and nutmeg.
4. Knead 1–2 minutes on floured board. Let stand 30 minutes.
5. Shape into rolls 1-inch-thick-by-2½-inches-long, using small amounts of flour to help shape. Let stand 15–30 minutes.
6. Drop into slowly boiling water. Remove with slotted spoon when gnocchi float to the top (about 3–4 minutes). Serve immediately with sweet butter and grated Parmesan cheese over the top. Makes 16.

These Italian spinach dumplings melt in your mouth. They're especially good as a first course to perk up the palate for the main dish. Letting the gnocchis set after you've formed them dries them out slightly and helps hold their shape when you boil them. A skillet is better than a saucepan for cooking these.

Gougère

½ C milk
2 T sweet butter, and butter for pan
½ C unbleached all-purpose flour
2 large eggs, room temperature
1 t Dijon-style prepared mustard
⅛ t white pepper
¼ t salt
⅓ C grated Parmesan cheese
⅓ C shredded Gruyère or Swiss cheese

1. Slowly bring milk and butter to a low boil in a heavy saucepan.
2. Stir in flour all at once and beat with a wooden spoon until dough forms into a ball. Dough should not stick to the spoon or pan. Remove from heat and cool 2–3 minutes.
3. Beat in eggs one at a time.
4. Add mustard, pepper, salt, ¼ C Parmesan, ¼ C Gruyère or Swiss cheese, and beat well.
5. Place dough in pastry bag with large fitting. Squeeze out dough in overlapping braids around the inside rim of a lightly buttered 8-inch cake pan.
6. Sprinkle remaining cheese mixture on top.
7. Bake at 425 degrees F. for 15 minutes. Reduce temperature to 325 degrees F. and bake another 20 minutes or until dark golden brown and firm. Serve warm. Serves 4.

This makes a delectable appetizer. It goes side by side with a good red Burgundy wine. The paste is a basic *pâté à chou* dough designed for many dishes, including—with sugar—cream puffs and chocolate eclairs. The shape suggested here is also used for a Paris–Brest, the large, round, whipped cream-filled pastry. The recipe may easily be doubled to make two gougères. Another classic rendition is to add some baked ham pieces. In this dish, when you are forming the gougère, squeeze out a ring of dough on a prepared baking sheet, another ring inside and touching the first, and a third on top of the crevice between the two. Then squeeze out eight small "dots" evenly spaced on the outside of the ring.

Haddock Pie

CRUST:

1   C unbleached all-purpose flour
½   t salt
1   t chopped dill
⅓   C shortening
4   T cold water

FILLING:

1   C flaked poached haddock
2   T olive oil
1   medium-sized onion, sliced thinly
¾   t salt
    dash of white pepper
¼   t thyme
3   oz. cream cheese, in small pieces
2   large tomatoes, peeled, de-seeded, sliced
2   large eggs
⅔   C light cream

1. For crust, mix flour, salt, and dill. Cut in shortening. Stir in water one T at a time until dough forms a ball. Roll out and place in 9-inch quiche pan. Pierce with fork. Bake at 450 degrees F. for 7–9 minutes or until lightly toasted. Cool.
2. For filling, place haddock in crust.
3. In skillet heat oil and sauté onion slices until transparent, not brown. Arrange over haddock.
4. Sprinkle on salt, pepper, and thyme. Scatter on cheese.
5. Arrange tomato slices over cheese.
6. Combine eggs and cream. Gently pour over tomatoes.
7. Bake at 350 degrees F. for 25 minutes or until lightly toasted and center is set. Serves 6.

Haddock may be cooked quickly by simmering it in milk or water; it's done when the fish is no longer transparent. Tomatoes may be easily peeled by first dropping them in boiling water for a minute or until the skin cracks. Then remove them to cold water and peel the skin. Scoop out the seeds with a spoon. Thyme belongs to the mint family, but is less obvious in aroma than the true mints. Nevertheless, a little goes a long way, and the taste works nicely with haddock.

Ham and Leek Quiche

CRUST:

1	C unbleached all-purpose flour
½	t salt
⅓	C shortening
3–4	T cold water

FILLING:

1	C diced baked ham
8	oz. shredded Gruyère cheese
3	T sweet butter
1	C sliced leeks
3	large eggs
1	pint light cream
¾	t salt
⅛	t white pepper
1	t dry mustard
⅛	t mace
	paprika

1. For crust, mix flour and salt. Cut in shortening. Stir in water one T at a time until dough forms a ball. Roll out and place in 9-inch quiche pan. Pierce with fork. Bake at 450 degrees F. for 7–9 minutes or until lightly toasted. Cool.

2. For filling, prepare ham and cheese and set aside.

3. Melt butter in large iron skillet. Sauté leeks until soft but not limp (about 10–15 minutes); place cover over skillet to steam leeks.

4. In bowl mix eggs and cream. Stir in salt, pepper, mustard, and mace.

5. Place ham and leeks in crust. Spread cheese over ham. Pour egg mixture over cheese. Sprinkle generously with paprika, especially in the center.

6. Bake at 350 degrees F. for 40 minutes or until the center is set. Serves 4–6.

Leeks are a choice member of the onion family. Their taste is subtle, never offensive, always appealing. Use primarily the white section from the root upward, and slice it thinly. Slicing some of the pale green section adds attractive spots of a lime-chartreuse color to the dish. Home-grown leeks take nearly the full season to mature, but they're easy to grow, occupy little space, and, plucked fresh from the garden, offer wonderful opportunities in a kitchen—from soups, to salads, to this quiche.

Hamburger Cheese Pie

CRUST:

- 1   C unbleached all-purpose flour
- ½   t salt
- 1   egg yolk
- 2–3   T cold milk

FILLING:

- ½   C chopped onion
- 1   clove garlic, minced
- 3   T olive oil
- 1½   lb. lean ground chuck
- ½   t oregano
- ¾   t salt
- ⅛   t freshly ground black pepper
- 1   large egg, slightly beaten
- 2   C cottage cheese
- 1   egg white, beaten until soft peaks form
- ½   C grated Swiss cheese paprika

1. For crust, mix flour and salt. Stir in egg yolk. Stir in milk one T at a time until dough forms a ball. Roll out and place in 9-inch pie plate. Pierce with fork. Bake at 450 degrees F. for 7–9 minutes or until lightly toasted. Cool.

2. For filling, use a small skillet to sauté onion and garlic in oil until transparent, not brown.

3. In separate larger skillet brown chuck. Drain excess fat, if any. Add oregano, salt, pepper, onion, and garlic.

4. Spoon meat mixture into crust.

5. Combine in small bowl egg and cottage cheese. Fold in egg white. Spoon over meat.

6. Bake at 375 degrees F. for 15 minutes. Sprinkle on Swiss cheese. Sprinkle the center decoratively with paprika. Bake 10 minutes more or until slightly toasted on top. Serve warm. Serves 4–6.

This dresses up ground chuck into a dish that, tried once, will probably reserve a permanent and frequent place in your quick kitchen repertoire. Placing the pie in a quiche pan dresses it up further. Be sure to brown the meat partially for a darker, hearty flavor.

Lobster Quiche

CRUST:

- 1 C unbleached all-purpose flour
- ½ t salt
- 3 T sweet butter
- 2 T shortening
- 3–4 T sour cream

FILLING:

- ¾ lb. lobster tail meat, cooked
- 1 T finely minced parsley
- ¾ t salt
- ⅛ t freshly ground black pepper
- ½ t dry mustard
- ½ t curry
- ⅓ C shredded Port Salut
- 2 T dry sherry
- 3 large eggs, slightly beaten
- 1½ C light cream
- paprika

1. For crust, mix flour and salt. Cut in butter and shortening. Stir in sour cream one T at a time until dough forms a ball. Chill. Roll out and place in 9-inch quiche pan. Pierce with fork. Bake at 450 degrees F. for 7–9 minutes or until lightly toasted. Cool.

2. For filling, combine lobster, parsley, salt, pepper, mustard, curry and cheese. Stir in sherry. Place in crust.

3. Blend eggs and cream. Pour over lobster mixture. Dust with paprika.

4. Bake at 350 degrees F. for 25 minutes or until toasted and center is set. Serves 6.

How can you beat fresh Maine lobster steamed in seaweed water and served with drawn butter, while the salt breezes from the crisp, bright Atlantic waft over a rocky coast? You can't. The old standbys of lobster Newburg and lobster Thermidor sauce up a food that is best left alone. Nevertheless, this quiche is for those who languish for lobster but can't get it fresh.

Macaroni Pie

1 C unbleached all-purpose
   flour
½ t salt
1 t chopped parsley
⅓ C shortening
4 T cold water

FILLING:
½ C macaroni, cooked
1½ C plum tomatoes, peeled
1 small onion, diced
1 clove garlic
2 T olive oil
2 sprigs sweet basil, chopped
¾ t salt
¼ t freshly ground black
   pepper
1 T tomato paste
¾ C cooked lean ground
   chuck
½ C shredded Bel Paese
   cheese
2 large eggs
½ C light cream
1 T grated Parmesan

1. For crust, mix flour, salt, and parsley. Cut in shortening. Stir in water one T at a time until dough forms a ball. Roll out and place in a high-sided 9-inch quiche pan. Pierce with fork. Bake at 450 degrees F. for 7–9 minutes or until lightly toasted. Cool.

2. For filling, prepare macaroni and set aside.

3. Peel tomatoes by first breaking skin in boiling water. Mash tomatoes in saucepan.

4. In skillet sauté onion and garlic in oil until transparent, not brown. Transfer to tomatoes. Add basil, salt, pepper, and tomato paste. Simmer for 20–30 minutes until thickened.

5. In skillet brown chuck. Place in crust.

6. Pour macaroni over chuck. Sprinkle on Bel Paese.

7. Combine eggs and cream. Pour over Bel Paese. Sprinkle on Parmesan. Bake at 350 degrees F. for 25 minutes or until center is set. Serves 6.

Pasta comes in all sorts of forms, from wire-thin vermicelli to broadleaf lasagne. Try to find ditalini for this dish. These are short stubby hollow tubes. Bel Paese is a mild soft cheese that gives a rich creamy undercoat to this savory pie.

Meatball Pie

CRUST:

1 C unbleached all-purpose
   flour
½ t salt
⅓ C shortening
4 T cold water

FILLING:

⅔ C unbleached all-purpose
   flour
¼ t baking powder
¾ t salt
¼ t black pepper, freshly
   ground
½ t coriander
1 medium-sized onion, diced
½ clove garlic, minced
2 T olive oil
3 large eggs
¾ lb. lean ground chuck
½ C sour cream
¾ C ricotta
   paprika

1. For crust, mix flour and salt. Cut in shortening. Stir in water one T at a time until dough forms a ball. Roll out and place in a 9-inch quiche pan. Pierce with fork. Bake at 450 degrees F. for 7–9 minutes or until lightly toasted. Cool.

2. For filling, mix flour, baking powder, salt, pepper, and coriander. Set aside.

3. Sauté onion and garlic in oil until transparent, not brown.

4. Mix 1 egg into chuck. Add onion and garlic mixture. Blend in the flour mixture.

5. Shape meat mixture into small teaspoon-sized balls. In an oiled iron skillet, brown meatballs. Place in crust.

6. Beat remaining 2 eggs, sour cream, and ricotta until smooth and light. Pour over meatballs. Sprinkle on paprika.

7. Bake at 350 degrees F. for 25 minutes or until nearly set. Serves 6.

When forming the meatballs, work lightly for better results. Don't pack the meat together. Just form it and the ball will hold together. If you wish a slightly spicier taste, increase the coriander. This seasoning, from the parsley family, is extremely versatile. It's used in sausage, breads, curry, cakes, and chilis. The restrained edge of coriander makes it much friendlier to use than some of the red-hot spices. This dish is good for a casual Friday night get-together or a Saturday afternoon lunch.

Meatloaf

butter for dish
¾ C bread crumbs
2 large eggs
¼ C light cream
1 lb. lean ground chuck
2 rashers lean bacon, broiled, crumbled finely
bacon fat
¼ C grated Parmesan
1 small onion, diced
1 T chopped parsley
1 t salt
¼ t freshly ground black pepper
1½ C ricotta
tomato sauce

1. Butter an 8 × 4 × 2-inch baking dish. Sprinkle on bread crumbs, reserving most of them. Set aside.
2. Mix 1 egg and cream into meat. Add bacon bits and fat, rest of bread crumbs, Parmesan, onion, parsley, salt, and pepper.
3. Thoroughly combine other egg with ricotta.
4. Place half of meat in dish. Spread on ricotta mixture. Carefully place on rest of meat mixture.
5. Brush with olive oil. Bake at 400 degrees F. for 20 minutes. Brush on a piquant tomato sauce. Continue baking another 10–15 minutes or until done. Turn onto platter and slice to serve. Serves 6–8.

Don't overcook this. Meatloaf is better moist. The background tastes of bacon and Parmesan cheese make this dish interesting. The color and lightness of the ricotta in the center add the flourish.

Mushroom Quiche

CRUST:

1 C unbleached all-purpose
   flour
½ t salt
⅓ C shortening
2 T chopped green scallion
   ends
4 T cold water

FILLING:

3 T sweet butter
8 oz. mushrooms, sliced
8 scallion greens, chopped
   ends
3 large eggs
4 T pimento, chopped
1 C thick buttermilk
¾ t salt
   white pepper to taste
1¼ C Swiss cheese grated

1. For crust, mix flour and salt. Cut in shortening. Stir in scallion ends. Stir in water one T at a time until dough forms a ball. Roll out and place in 9-inch quiche pan. Pierce with fork. Bake at 450 degrees F. for 7–9 minutes or until lightly toasted. Cool.

2. For filling, melt butter in large skillet. Sauté mushrooms until their moisture nearly evaporates, about 7–8 minutes.

3. Add scallions that have been chopped from the white end and at least 1 inch into the green section before the leaves separate. Sauté another 5–6 minutes.

4. In mixing bowl beat eggs slightly. Add pimento, buttermilk, salt, and pepper, and mix well.

5. Spread cheese onto bottom of crust.

6. Carefully pour egg mixture over cheese.

7. Bake at 375 degrees F. for 25 minutes or until center is set and toasted lightly. Serves 4–6.

The pimento provides not only a festive red flair to the quiche, but also a mellow, pleasing complement to the predominant mushroom taste. This dish is especially enjoyable for lunch on an uncomplicated day that calls for something tasty but not overpowering.

Olive Quiche

CRUST:
1   C cornflake crumbs
3   T sweet butter, melted

FILLING:
½   T unflavored gelatin
¼   C cold water
8   oz. cream cheese, softened
1   T mild prepared mustard
2   T mayonnaise
½   C pitted ripe black olives,
     chopped
3   T chopped pimento
¼   C chopped walnuts

1. For crust, mix crumbs and butter. Press into bottom and up side of 9-inch quiche pan. Bake at 450 degrees F. for 4 minutes or until set. Cool.

2. For filling, sprinkle gelatin over water in a saucepan and soak for 5 minutes. Stir over medium heat until dissolved.

3. Beat together cheese, mustard, mayonnaise, and gelatin until smooth. Stir in olives, pimento, and walnuts.

4. Carefully spread over crust. Chill for 3 hours. Serves 8–10.

Cut as hors d'oeuvre or appetizers, this felicitous combination of chopped black olives and cream cheese makes a surprisingly pleasant dish. It's a takeoff from the old-time olive and cream cheese sandwich, which, like this quiche, is a quick and novel dish to prepare.

Onion Quiche

CRUST:

1	C unbleached all-purpose flour
½	t salt
1	egg yolk
3	T shortening
3–4	T cold milk

FILLING:

5	yellow medium-sized onions
¼	C sweet butter
1	T olive oil
¾	t salt
⅛	t white pepper
2	t paprika
3	oz. cream cheese, softened
3	large eggs, slightly beaten
1	C light cream
½	C sour cream

1. For crust, mix flour and salt. Stir in egg yolk. Cut in shortening. Stir in milk one T at a time until dough forms a ball. Chill. Roll out and place in 9-inch quiche pan. Pierce with fork. Bake at 450 degrees F. for 7–9 minutes or until lightly toasted. Cool.

2. For filling, peel and slice onions into rather large pieces.

3. In large iron skillet melt butter in oil. Sauté onions until transparent, not brown.

4. Add salt, pepper, and paprika.

5. Spread mixture on crust.

6. Beat cheese until smooth and light. Mix in eggs and creams. Pour over onions.

7. Bake at 375 degrees F. for 40 minutes or until center is set. Serves 6.

If you've tried everything from match sticks in your mouth to goggles to keep onions from making you tear while you peel them, here's a tip that really works: Hold the onions under running water as you peel them. Adding a little oil to the butter prevents the butter from burning brown, allowing you to sauté at a higher temperature. This simple quiche has a mild taste that may accompany stronger dishes.

Pizza

CRUST:
1   T dry yeast
¾   C warm water
    pinch of sugar
½   t salt
1¾ C unbleached all-purpose
    flour, with extra flour for
    kneading
    oil for bowl

FILLING:
2   C Italian plum tomatoes
2   T olive oil
1   T parsley, minced
½   t oregano
1   clove garlic, minced
2   T tomato paste
¾   t salt
⅛   t black pepper, freshly
    ground
    pepperoni slices
½   C black olives, sliced
¾   lb. Mozzarella cheese,
    grated

1. For crust, dissolve yeast in water. Add sugar and salt. Stir in half of flour and beat 1 minute. Add rest of flour. Place on board and knead 8–10 minutes, adding flour to prevent stickiness. Cover in oiled bowl and let rise in warm place until doubled in bulk (about 45 minutes). Punch down and roll out to make two 8-inch or 1 large 9 × 12-inch pizza.
2. For filling, crush tomatoes in saucepan. Add oil, parsley, oregano, and garlic, and cook 5 minutes over medium-high heat.
3. Reduce heat to simmer and blend in tomato paste. Continue simmering to thicken sauce, about 20 minutes. Add salt and pepper.
4. Pour sauce into crust. Place on desired number of pepperoni slices. Add olives and sprinkle on cheese.
5. Bake at 400 degrees F. for 20–30 minutes or until cheese and crust rim are lightly toasted. Serves 4–6.

You may urge on the yeast to work by placing the bowl with the dough in another bowl containing hot water. Pizza is an open-ended dish, and may contain any reasonable combination of ingredients— sausage, bacon, green pepper slices, mushrooms. The Mozzarella may be thinly sliced instead of grated, and put over the sauce. Placed in round cake pans, pizzas may be frozen with no harm done, and will be ready for cooking on short notice.

Pork and Apple Cheese Pie

CRUST:

2   C unbleached all-purpose flour
1   t salt
⅔   C shortening
4–6   T cold water

FILLING:

2   C cooked pork shoulder, shredded
    apple cider vinegar to cover
1   small onion, chopped
1   T olive oil
1   large tart cooking apple, peeled, cored, sliced
½   t salt
½   t mace
½   t coriander
2   T brown sugar
1   C shredded Bel Paese cheese
    egg white

1. For crust, mix flour and salt. Cut in shortening. Stir in water one T at a time until dough forms a ball. Cut in half. Roll out half and place on 9-inch pie plate. Reserve the other half for the top.

2. For filling, marinate pork in vinegar for 1 hour.

3. Sauté onion in oil until transparent, not brown.

4. Combine apple with salt, mace, coriander, and sugar. Stir in onions.

5. Drain and dry pork. Combine with apple mixture. Place snugly into crust.

6. Sprinkle on cheese.

7. Roll out second crust and place securely over mixture, fluting edge decoratively. Cut crescent in center of crust and pierce the rest decoratively with a fork. Brush with egg white.

8. Bake at 450 degrees F. for 10 minutes. Reduce temperature to 350 degrees F. and continue baking for another 30 minutes or until crust is lightly toasted. Serves 6.

Marinating the pork in vinegar gives this a light, sweet-and-sour undertaste when combined with the brown sugar. The apples keep the pie moist. Meat and fruit are good friends, and should get together like this more often.

Potato Cheese Pie I

butter for dish
⅓ C bread crumbs
3 potatoes, peeled, boiled
2 T chopped dill
3 large eggs, hard boiled,
  sliced
salt and pepper to taste
½ C baked cubed ham
4 oz. cream cheese, softened
4 oz. sour cream
¾ C light cream
2 T sweet butter, melted
paprika

1. Butter bottom and side of 1½-quart baking dish and coat with half of bread crumbs.
2. Slice potatoes thinly. Place ½ of the potatoes and 1 T dill in the dish. Place ½ of the egg slices over the potatoes. Shake on salt and pepper to taste. Then sprinkle ½ of the ham over eggs. Repeat, laying on the remaining potatoes, dill, and egg, ending with ham.
3. Beat cheese and creams together. Pour over potato layers.
4. Mix remaining bread crumbs and butter. Sprinkle over potatoes. Dust with paprika.
5. Bake at 350 degrees F. for 20 minutes or until lightly toasted but not dry. Serves 4–6.

Paprika is the ground powder of a red pepper. Most paprika is mild, nearly bland, and is used more for its color and eye-appeal than for its taste. Hungarian paprika is noted for its flavor. All paprika must be kept very fresh and bright red. This dish makes tasty use of sour cream, another Hungarian favorite.

Potato Cheese Pie II

CRUST:
½ C bread crumbs
¼ C grated sharp Cheddar
    cheese
¼ t salt
½ t paprika
    butter for pie plate

FILLING:
4 large potatoes, peeled and
    boiled
½ C light cream
¼ C sweet butter, in pieces
1 large egg, separated
¼ C chopped fresh parsley
¼ C chopped fresh basil
½ t salt
⅛ t white pepper
½ lb. Mozzarella cheese, sliced
    thinly
½ C grated Parmesan cheese
    butter
    paprika

1. For crust, mix crumbs, cheese, salt, and paprika. Butter a 9-inch pie plate. Sprinkle and gently press mixture onto plate.

2. For filling, mash potatoes by hand (do not purée). Stir in cream, butter, and egg yolk.

3. Whip egg white until stiff. Fold into potatoes.

4. Blend in parsley, basil, salt, and pepper.

5. Spread one-third of potato mixture gently over crumbs. Cover with Mozzarella slices. Continue in alternate layers, ending with Mozzarella.

6. Sprinkle top with Parmesan. Dot with butter. Sprinkle with paprika.

7. Bake at 350 degrees F. for 45 minutes or until top is toasted. Serves 6.

Good fresh Mozzarella, made with skim milk, fits the simple taste of potatoes and herbs. No onion or garlic in this one. The grated Parmesan, a hard cheese, adds just enough subtle strength.

Quiche Lorraine

CRUST:

    1   C unbleached all-purpose
        flour
    ½   t salt
    1   large egg, slightly beaten
    4   T sweet butter
  3–4   T cold milk

FILLING:

    ¼   lb. shredded Port Salut
        cheese
    1   T finely chopped onion
    ½   C diced smoked, cooked
        ham
    3   egg yolks
    1   whole egg
    ⅛   t salt
    ½   t dry mustard
    1   t Dijon mustard
        dash of cayenne
    ¼   t freshly ground nutmeg
   1¾   C light cream

1. For crust, mix flour and salt. Stir in egg. Cut in butter. Stir in milk one T at a time until dough forms a ball. Chill. Roll out and place in 9-inch quiche pan. Pierce with fork. Bake at 450 degrees F. for 7–9 minutes or until lightly toasted. Cool.

2. For filling, combine cheese, onion, and ham. Sprinkle over bottom of crust.

3. Blend egg yolks, whole egg, salt, mustards, cayenne, and nutmeg.

4. Stir in cream. Pour mixture over cheese mixture.

5. Bake at 350 degrees F. for 40 minutes or until thoroughly set. Serve hot. Serves 4–6.

Just as the thick-textured New York style typifies cheesecakes, so does this quiche Lorraine typify cheese pies. Port Salut cheese was created by Trappist monks at the Port-du-Salut monastery in Entrammes, France. The cheese comes in four-pound rounds covered with an inedible orange rind. St. Paulin cheese substitutes well for the Port Salut. A mild Swiss style cheese may also be used with good result in this quiche. The top of the quiche should be richly toasted. You may test whether this and other quiches are set by inserting a knife in the center of the custard. If the knife comes out clean, the quiche is done.

Roquefort Quiche

CRUST:
- 1 C unbleached all-purpose flour
- ½ t salt
- ⅓ C shortening
- 3–4 T sour cream

FILLING:
- ⅓ C Roquefort cheese, crumpled
- 4 large eggs, slightly beaten
- 1 C light cream
- ½ C sour cream
- ½ t salt
- ⅛ t white pepper
- 1 T chopped dill
- 2 T Cognac

1. For crust, mix flour and salt. Cut in shortening. Stir in sour cream one T at a time until dough forms a ball. Chill. Roll out and place in 9-inch quiche pan. Pierce with fork. Bake at 450 degrees F. for 7–9 minutes or until lightly toasted. Cool.

2. For filling, place Roquefort in crust.

3. Blend eggs, light and sour creams. Stir in salt, pepper, dill, and Cognac.

4. Pour over Roquefort. Bake at 350 degrees F. for 25 minutes or until lightly toasted and center is set. Serves 6–8.

Roquefort is known as the "King of Cheeses." American cow's milk imitations have the blue veins but not the unique taste of real Roquefort. It's made in limestone caves in the French village of the same name and is said to be impossible to duplicate elsewhere. Roquefort is made from ewe's milk, and is identified by the red sheep label on the five-pound, foil-wrapped cheese. This dish is rich and hearty-flavored and is best served as an hors d'oeuvre.

Salmon Pie

CRUST:

2   C unbleached all-purpose
     flour
1   t salt
6   T sweet butter
4   T shortening
4–6 T cold water

FILLING:

2   T sweet butter, melted
1   pear, peeled, cored, sliced
1   apple, peeled, cored, sliced
¾   C white wine
     juice of 1 fresh lemon
¼   t salt
⅛   t cloves
⅛   t mace
¼   t coriander
⅓   C raisins
5   prunes, diced
3   dates, diced
3   dried figs, diced
½   lb. red salmon
½   C ricotta
¼   C sour cream
¼   C light cream
     milk or egg white

1. For crust, mix flour and salt. Cut in butter and shortening. Stir in water one T at a time until dough forms a ball. Chill. Roll out half and place in 9-inch pie plate. Cover and set aside second half for top crust.

2. For filling, melt butter in skillet. Coat pear and apple slices with butter. Add wine and lemon juice. Cover skillet and simmer for 10 minutes.

3. Remove slices and combine them with salt, cloves, mace, coriander, raisins, prunes, dates, figs, and salmon.

4. Place compactly in crust.

5. Blend ricotta and creams. Pour over filling.

6. Roll out top crust and place over filling, fluting edges. Brush with milk or egg white.

7. Bake at 450 degrees F. for 10 minutes. Reduce temperature to 350 degrees F. and continue baking another 30 minutes or until crust is toasted. Serves 6.

Based on a medieval recipe, this pie combines what are too seldom joined—fish and fruit. The pie is chock-full of tastes that challenge identification—and yet overall a balance is achieved. The natural sugar in the fruits tilts the pie toward the sweet side, but the salmon keeps the rudder angling this for a savory dish.

Scallop Yogurt Quiche

CRUST:

  1 C unbleached all-purpose
      flour
  ½ t salt
  5 T shortening
3–4 T cold water

FILLING:

  3 rashers lean bacon, diced
  1 medium-sized white onion,
      chopped
  3 large eggs, slightly beaten
  1 C plain yogurt
  ½ lb. fresh bay scallops
  2 T fresh chives, minced
  2 T brandy
  ¼ t salt
  ⅛ t white pepper
  ½ C shredded Swiss cheese
      paprika

1. For crust, mix flour and salt. Cut in shortening. Stir in water one T at a time to form dough into a ball. Roll out and place in 9-inch quiche pan. Pierce with fork. Bake at 450 degrees F. for 7–9 minutes or until lightly toasted.

2. For filling, fry bacon in large iron skillet. Remove with slotted spoon, leaving fat in skillet. Set bacon pieces aside.

3. Sauté onion lightly in skillet until transparent, not brown.

4. Mix eggs, yogurt, scallops, chives, brandy. Stir in salt and pepper.

5. Sprinkle bacon, onion, and cheese evenly over bottom of crust.

6. Pour on scallop-yogurt mixture. Sprinkle heavily with paprika.

7. Bake at 350 degrees F. for 40 minutes or until center is set. Serves 4–6.

Bay or Cape scallops are bite-sized, perfect in their size and sweet taste for this quiche. Sea scallops are three and four times larger, and may be used, but first they should be cut into thirds. If you have trouble finding scallops, use instead, in priority, fresh bay scallops, frozen bay, fresh sea, and finally frozen sea scallops. Yogurt makes a surprisingly pleasing custard base and may be used in many other recipes calling for at least three eggs.

Seafood Quiche

CRUST:

1 C unbleached all-purpose
   flour
½ t salt
2 T sweet butter
3 T shortening
4 T cold milk

FILLING:

2   T sweet butter
1   small onion, minced
2   T brandy
1   t chopped fresh chives
½   t dried thyme
¼   lb. bay scallops
½   lb. sole, in small pieces
½   lb. crabmeat, shredded
4   eggs
2   C light cream
4–5 drops hot sauce
½   t curry
     salt and pepper to taste
3   T grated Parmesan
     paprika

1. For crust, mix flour and salt. Cut in butter and shortening. Stir in milk one T at a time to form dough into a ball. Chill. Roll out and place in 9-inch quiche pan. Pierce with fork. Bake at 450 degrees F. for 7–9 minutes or until lightly toasted. Cool.

2. For filling, melt butter in heavy iron skillet. Sauté onion until transparent, not brown.

3. Remove skillet from heat and add brandy, chives, thyme. Mix in scallops, sole, and crab.

4. In separate bowl beat eggs lightly. Stir in cream, hot sauce, curry, salt, and pepper.

5. Combine seafood and egg mixtures. Pour into crust.

6. Sprinkle top with Parmesan and paprika. Bake at 350 degrees F. for 25 minutes or until center is set. Serves 6.

Just about any combination of fish makes an interesting catchall seafood quiche. Lobster, shrimp, cusk, even finnan haddie (smoked haddock) may be substituted to good effect. This makes a hearty dish with distinctive flavors from the sea.

Spaghetti Cheese Pie

SAUCE:

6–7 large fresh tomatoes,
     peeled, mashed
  2 t oregano
  3 T olive oil
  1 clove garlic, finely minced
  2 T tomato paste
    salt and pepper to taste

FILLING:

 ½ lb. lean ground chuck
1½ C water
  4 oz. spaghetti
  8 oz. ricotta
  1 large egg
  1 T fresh chopped parsley
 ½ t salt
 ½ t oregano
  1 clove garlic, minced
  4 oz. shredded Mozzarella
    cheese
    grated Parmesan cheese

1. For sauce, combine all ingredients and cook until slightly thickened.

2. For filling, brown beef in large saucepan.

3. Stir in spaghetti sauce and water. Bring to boil. Add spaghetti. Cover and cook over medium heat 5–7 minutes or until tender. Stir occasionally.

4. In bowl mix ricotta, egg, parsley, salt, oregano, and garlic.

5. Spread half the spaghetti into 9-inch pie plate.

6. Top with ricotta cheese mixture.

7. Put the rest of the spaghetti mixture on top. Sprinkle with Mozzarella cheese. Then sprinkle with grated Parmesan.

8. Bake at 350 degrees F. for 20 minutes or until top is lightly toasted.

9. Remove from oven and let stand about 5 minutes. Serves 6.

This turns inexpensive ingredients into a tasty new form. The Mozzarella melts and spreads over the top like a crust, hiding the spaghetti and making a nice surprise if the pie is served at the table. With hot crusty Italian bread and a bright green romaine lettuce salad, the dish adds a welcome variation on an old friendly theme.

Spinach Cheese Pie

- 1   lb. phyllo sheets
- ¾   C sweet butter, melted, and butter for dish

FILLING:
- 2   lbs. fresh spinach, washed, de-stemmed
- 1   lb. feta cheese, drained to de-salt
- 3   oz. cream cheese, softened
- 3   scallions, chopped
- ½   t dill weed
- 4   large eggs, slightly beaten

1. For crust, spread ⅓ of phyllo in a buttered 12 × 8 × 2-inch baking dish, brushing each sheet with melted butter. Cover rest of phyllo with damp cloth to prevent drying.
2. For filling, boil down water-sprinkled spinach until tender. Squeeze out water. Chop spinach only slightly.
3. Blend in cheeses. Mix in scallions and dill.
4. Blend in eggs.
5. Spread half the filling on the phyllo. Place ⅓ of phyllo on filling, brushing each sheet with melted butter. Repeat.
6. With a sharp knife, score the top phyllo layer only into large diamond sections. Brush top with cold water.
7. Bake at 350 degrees F. for 45 minutes or until toasted. Rest the pie 5 minutes before serving. Serves 6.

A *mezzaluna* (a rounded blade with two handles) is a good utensil for many uses, including chopping spinach. As in all recipes suggesting phyllo, sprinkling water on top helps to prevent the top sheets from curling while the dish bakes. When cutting phyllo, dip a knife in hot water for easier cutting. This spinach pie is known as *spanakopita*, a favorite Greek dish.

Spinach Quiche

CRUST:

1¼ C unbleached all-purpose
     flour
½   t salt
3   T sweet butter
3   T shortening
1   egg yolk
3–4 T cold water

FILLING:

1   clove garlic, minced
1   medium-sized onion, diced
4   T olive oil, divided
1   C fresh zucchini, chopped
½   C green pepper, de-seeded,
     de-stemmed, chopped
3   large eggs, slightly beaten
1½ C cottage cheese
3   oz. cream cheese,
     softened, diced
½   t salt
⅛   t black pepper, freshly
     ground
1   t dill weed
½   t freshly ground nutmeg
10 oz. spinach, cooked,
     drained, chopped
⅓   C grated Parmesan cheese
½   C all-purpose cream

1. For crust, mix flour and salt. Cut in butter and shortening. Stir in egg yolk. Add cold water one T at a time to form dough into ball. Chill. Roll out and place in high-sided 9-inch quiche pan. Pierce with fork. Bake at 450 degrees F. for 7–9 minutes or until lightly toasted. Cool.

2. For filling, sauté garlic and onion in 2 T oil until transparent, not brown. Remove and set aside.

3. In 2 T oil sauté zucchini and green pepper until slightly tender. Combine with onion mixture.

4. In separate bowl mix eggs with cottage cheese. Add cream cheese and, if necessary, slice in with pastry cutter.

5. Add salt, pepper, dill, and nutmeg.

6. To cheese mixture add onion mixture. Then add spinach, Parmesan, and cream. Mix well.

7. Pour into crust. Bake at 350 degrees F. for 40 minutes or until center is set. Remove quiche pan side and serve hot. Serves 6.

This is an irresistible quiche. It may be served as a main course or, cut into thinner wedges, as an appetizer. It turns out relatively thick, is a dark, inviting green, and tastes surprisingly creamy and flavorful. The vegetables blend well in taste and have subtle differences in textures. It's a straightforward, winning dish.

Succotash Pie

CRUST:

1 C unbleached all-purpose
   flour
½ t salt
⅓ C shortening
4 T cold water

FILLING:

1½ C freshly cut corn
¾ C chopped green pepper
2 T olive oil
¼ C chopped pimento
1 C ricotta
1 large egg, slightly beaten
¾ t salt
⅛ t white pepper

1. For crust, mix flour and salt. Cut in shortening. Stir in water one T at a time until dough forms a ball. Roll out and place in 9-inch quiche pan. Pierce with fork. Bake at 450 degrees F. for 7–9 minutes or until lightly toasted. Cool.
2. For filling, sauté corn and pepper in oil in large iron skillet. Stirring constantly, cook until only slightly tender. Add pimento and remove from heat.
3. Mix ricotta and egg. Stir in salt and pepper.
4. Combine ricotta and corn mixtures. Pour into crust.
5. Bake at 350 degrees F. for 25 minutes or until center is set and lightly toasted. Serves 6.

Authentic succotash is a simple combination of fresh sweet corn cut from the cob and lima beans, but the name fits this variation, too, if only to conjure a summery vegetable dish that needs no further invitation than its sight to enjoy anytime.

Tamale Pie

CRUST:

1 C masa harina
½ t salt
½ t cumin
⅓ C shortening
½ C water

FILLING:

1 lb. lean ground chuck
1 large onion, diced
1 clove garlic, minced
2 T olive oil
2 C tomatoes
2 C whole sweet corn
1 T hot chili sauce
2 t chili powder
1 t salt
⅛ t freshly ground black
    pepper
1 t cumin
½ C black olives, sliced in
    quarters
1 C shredded Cheddar cheese

1. For crust, mix masa harina, salt, and cumin. Cut in shortening. Stir in water a little at a time until the mixture is pourable. Set aside.
2. For filling, brown the chuck in an iron skillet.
3. In separate skillet, sauté onion and garlic in oil until transparent, not brown.
4. Place tomatoes and corn (and their juices) in large saucepan. Stir in chili sauce, chili powder, salt, pepper, and cumin. Simmer.
5. Add chuck, onion, and garlic to tomato mixture. Cook covered for 20 minutes.
6. Pour into 12 × 8 × 2-inch baking dish. Press in olives. Sprinkle on cheese.
7. Add enough water to masa harina to make it pourable, if it has become too thick. Carefully spoon on masa harina mixture (it doesn't need to cover the filling completely).
8. Bake at 350 degrees F. for 40 minutes or until crust is lightly toasted and set. Serves 6–8.

The crust may also be placed in the bottom of the dish first with the top left open or covered with additional masa harina. Masa harina, traditional in Mexico, is finely ground corn flour that has been treated with lime water. It is used for tamales, tortillas, and other dishes. Masa harina gives the characteristic Mexican taste. If it is difficult to find, fine yellow cornmeal works similarly. The amount of chili in this recipe is mildly hot, so you may judge your own rendition by either a lighter or heavier hand on the measuring spoons.

Tomato Cheese Pie

CRUST:
- 1   C unbleached all-purpose flour
- ½   t salt
- 5   T sweet butter
- 1   egg yolk
- 2–3 T cold milk

FILLING:
- 3   large tomatoes
- ¼   t salt
- ⅛   t pepper
- 1   t oregano
- 3–4 T olive oil
- ½   lb. Fontina cheese
- 1   t prepared mustard

1. For crust, mix flour and salt. Cut in butter. Stir in egg yolk. Stir in milk one T at a time to form dough into ball. Chill. Roll out and place in 9-inch quiche pan. Pierce with fork. Bake at 450 degrees F. for 7–9 minutes or until lightly toasted.

2. For filling, slice tomatoes in ½-inch thick rounds. Remove ends, liquid, and seeds from slices.

3. Place slices on platter. Sprinkle on salt, pepper, and oregano. Pour on oil. Set aside.

4. Slice cheese into ⅛-inch-thick sections. Place ample cheese over bottom of crust.

5. Brush on mustard.

6. Place tomato slices decoratively over cheese. Pour on oil from platter.

7. Bake at 350 degrees F. for 35 minutes or until done. Serves 6–8.

The jolly-looking tomato once carried a nefarious reputation. Known as the wolf peach, love apple, and lethal aphrodisiac, the benign New World tomato suffered ignominy from the general public (except by enlightened Thomas Jefferson) until as late as 1830, when daring Col. Robert Johnson of Salem, Massachusetts, ate a basketful in public and finally turned the tide. Medical predictions for Johnson were that he would foam at the mouth, suffer brain fever, or—if he lasted long enough—develop stomach cancer. He didn't, and neither will you with this simple but melodic tomato-cheese combination.

Vegetable Quiche

CRUST:

1   C unbleached all-purpose
     flour
½   t salt
3   T chopped dill
⅓   C shortening
4   T cold water

FILLING:

1   clove garlic, minced
3   T diced onion
⅓   C diced carrots
⅓   C diced celery
¼   C freshly cut corn
¼   C diced green pepper
¼   C diced potato
3–4 T olive oil
4   large eggs, slightly beaten
2   C all-purpose cream
1½   C shredded Swiss cheese
¼   t salt
      dash of white pepper
¼   t coriander
      paprika

1. For crust, mix flour, salt, and dill. Cut in shortening. Stir in water one T at a time until dough forms a ball. Roll out and place in 9-inch quiche pan. Pierce with fork. Bake at 450 degrees F. for 7–9 minutes or until lightly toasted. Cool.

2. For filling, sauté all vegetables in oil until slightly tender. Don't overcook.

3. Remove from skillet and spread on crust.

4. Mix eggs, cream, cheese, salt, pepper, and coriander. Pour over vegetables.

5. Sprinkle center generously with paprika.

6. Bake at 325 degrees F. for 45 minutes or until center is set. Cool 5 minutes before cutting. Serves 6–8.

This is an open-ended quiche. Virtually any combination of vegetables works, but try to keep them uniform in size. You might try asparagus, artichoke hearts, broccoli, peas. As always, including bright colors increases the eye-appeal of the dish.

Yam and Apricot Pie

CRUST:

1 C unbleached all-purpose flour
½ t salt
⅓ C shortening
4 T cold water
egg white

FILLING:

½ C dried apricots, rehydrated
2 C yams, cooked and cubed
3 T orange juice
3 T sweet butter, melted
⅓ t cinnamon
2 T dark brown sugar
1 C cottage cheese
sweet butter

TOPPING:

sour cream, thinned slightly with milk

1. For crust, mix flour and salt. Cut in shortening. Stir in water one T at a time until dough forms a ball. Roll out and place in 9-inch pie plate. Brush the bottom with egg white. Pierce with fork. Bake at 450 degrees F. for 7–9 minutes or until lightly toasted. Cool.

2. For filling, cut the apricots about the same size as the yam cubes. Combine in a bowl.

3. Stir in orange juice, butter, cinnamon, and sugar.

4. Spread cottage cheese on bottom of crust. Carefully place yam mixture over cheese. Dot with butter.

5. Bake at 350 degrees F. for 30 minutes or until top is lightly toasted.

6. For topping, drape sour cream over slices. Serves 6.

This mellow-colored, mellow-tasting pie adds a fitting tone to a casual autumn dinner table. If you can rehydrate the apricots (either soaking overnight or cooking them) with orange juice, all the better. Just as you might serve acorn squash with a little brown sugar and slabs of sweet butter as an accompaniment to a main course, try serving this pie on the side, too.

Yogurt Quiche

CRUST:
1   C unbleached
      all-purpose flour
¾   t salt
3   T sweet butter
3   T shortening
4   T cold milk

FILLING:
½   C mushrooms, sliced
1   onion, diced
3   T sweet butter
3   large eggs, slightly beaten
½   C plain yogurt
½   C light cream
½   t salt
      dash of white pepper
1½ C shredded Swiss cheese
10 rashers lean bacon, broiled
      and crumpled

1. For crust, mix flour and salt. Cut in butter and shortening. Stir in milk one T at a time until dough forms a ball. Chill. Roll out and place in 9-inch quiche pan. Pierce with fork. Bake at 450 degrees F. for 7–9 minutes or until lightly toasted. Cool.

2. For filling, sauté mushrooms and onion in butter until soft.

3. Blend eggs, yogurt, cream, salt, and pepper.

4. Cover crust with cheese. Sprinkle cheese with bacon, mushrooms, and onions.

5. Pour on egg mixture.

6. Bake at 350 degrees F. for 35 minutes or until center is set. Serves 6.

Mushrooms have little to recommend them for nutrition, but their presence adds a subtle pungent flavor to everything from soups to quiches. Mushrooms that you see in both market and woods are the fruits of a fungus growing underground. Use only the freshest white cap mushrooms. Don't overcook them or they will toughen.

INDEX